How to Live with a Working Wife

Jim Douglas is a middle-aged housewife living in the home counties with two children, cat, dog and a working wife. Once he was a managing director and went on business trips and had to be called out of meetings to visit his family. Now his wife works and goes away on trips. But when she is at home she looks after things so most of this book is a cheat really. However, it is true (as the book suggests) that he likes vodka and Gauloises and kicks the dog.

D0525288

Jim Douglas

How to Live with a Working Wife

The husband's guide to household arts

with illustrations by the author

Pan Original
Pan Books London and Sydney

First published 1983 by Pan Books Ltd,
Cavaye Place, London SW10 9PG
© Jim Douglas 1983
ISBN 0 330 28092 9

Phototypeset by Input Typesetting Ltd
Printed in Great Britain by
Richard Clay (The Chaucer Press) Ltd,
Bungay, Suffolk

This book is sold subject to the condition that it
shall not, by way of trade or otherwise, be lent, re-sold,
hired out, or otherwise circulated without the publisher's prior
consent in any form of binding or cover other than that in which
it is published and without a similar condition including this
condition being imposed on the subsequent purchaser

Contents

Tables

Technical checklists

Philosophical introduction

IF YOU LIVE with a working wife, you are probably a husband, and this book is primarily addressed to you.

Only husbands have wives, but not only husbands live with wives. Children, in-laws and pets live with wives. These other categories of being may be more or less sentient, or sensitive, than husbands and, if they can read, may benefit from some (but not all) of the following chapters.

Wives have to live with themselves and, if a mirror is offered to them, they usually choose to look in it. They also live with their husbands and should be interested if there is some possibility of change occurring in their companion. You may have noticed that a real change of life-style is unusual and difficult. One's personality becomes fixed, and habits deeply ingrained.

This book is also aimed at an imbalance in the current output of semi-serious, semi-facetious sexist literature concerned with the difficulties of the woman's lot. Any man who has tried to dress children, wash them, feed them, take them to school, collect them from school, buy their clothes, wash them, mend them, buy food, cook it, serve it, keep the house clean, keep himself clean, fragrant, smiling, will know how time-consuming, exhausting and often stultifying the process is. If he has to go and work more or less full time some distance away, certain physical impossibilities arise, such as being in two places at once. Then he gets involved in a further level of arrangements and anxieties.

We wanted to start from a different place. We know that husbands often take all the above for granted, that they escape with relief to their work, and play their various competitive games with each other. We believe that women should be able to go out into adult society and make some money, or do something interesting, or both.

But some perspective is required. Wife and husband alike are trapped by social patterns and conventions. If the wife is a slave to the household, the husband is the slave of his employer. Many husbands come to loathe the unremitting financial responsibility. But society is organised against revolution. Usually the husband cannot work flexibly, nor is the wife's earning power enough to replace his contribution.

The seed of change is within the home. The frustrated wife will get more satisfaction by persuading (or even forcing) change upon her husband than by public protestation of sexist injustice. Husbands and wives should try to be friendly to each other and accept that neither of them is free, that both were long ago set upon more or less predictable courses by external circumstances, and that both have a duty in life to make of themselves and their children something better than when they started.

If you have a working wife, you have a lot to put up with, and a lot to learn. This book gives some practical guidelines – some superficial, some frivolous, a few (between the lines) serious – on how to play your part in your household.

Some husbands want to help in the home; others have to. The hero of our book is obviously around the house quite a lot. It isn't clear, and it doesn't matter, whether he works or doesn't work, or works from home, or works sometimes, or what. You do what you can.

Remember that you can't change others, but you have a small chance of changing your own attitudes to things and the way you do them.

Life is full of absurdities and, if you step aside from daily pretenc you have to laugh or cry at human nature. The best course is to be compassionate to others, and to laugh at your own fate.

1
Fitting it all in
or
Organisation, timetables and a profound sense of fulfilment

NOTHING IN your previous existence prepared you for this. Culture shock is an understatement. You might experience surprise, or professional frustration, or intellectual deprivation if you had time. You are a numb sacrifice to the lives of others. The next generation is already walking on your grave.

You, poor devil, are in charge of the house. You are in charge of the family. Your wife goes out to work, you may even try to go out and work as well.

Formerly you may have gone off in the mornings, come home at night, everything was more or less organised, even welcoming; the children had been to school and were home again, your shirt was washed, the rubbish had been put out. And off you went to work again. You knew where you were. You had a particular job and you did it. Your mates let you do it. You might even have been in charge of something. You had a secretary. You got her to do things for you. She did them. You could call people and ask them to come and see you and do things for you. You were paid for doing this.

Now you are at home, even if you aren't there all the time. Perhaps your wife helps you, or you help her. But it's another world.

You're responsible for it but you're not really in charge of it. You don't run it, it runs you. You can't order it around. Even your children only partially do what you say. There is too much to do.

The timetable isn't your idea. You have to get on with people in a sort of social free-for-all where things aren't cut and dried and you don't have any particular position.

And money – forget it. You need money every day. But where does it come from? More to the point, where does other people's money come from? *They* always seem to have some, even if you don't. Now you're a housewife, you can begin to live with that hopeless, helpless feeling about money. You haven't got any, you can't earn any, you are just not in control. On Mondays you can collect the child allowance. You begin thinking about pin money.

Perhaps you are luckier than this. A lot of people aren't.

Getting used to it

The hardest thing about becoming a housewife and housekeeper is the transitional period. Men sometimes have to look after the home temporarily while their wives are away. Then you have to learn the routine and the timetable and remember all the trivial but vital details, especially with children, like dinner money and music lessons. By the time you have had a couple of weeks of it, the timetable has sunk in and what's more you've got to grips with your own way of organising things and buying food and washing clothes. Then your wife comes back and takes over again and you forget a lot of it.

The hardest thing is feeling you have to do things the way your wife wants them. That way you always feel under pressure and you're racking your brains in case you've forgotten something. Then she comes home and asks if you ran the woollens on full spin. Again.

Instead of this you have to find a way of acting as if it's your house and you're in charge. Then you begin to feel free. And *then* you can begin to draw some enjoyment from what you have to do anyway.

You realise – slowly you realise – that you have to get organised. It occurs to you that your wife, when she was doing it all, was remarkably well organised. The other mothers you meet now must be quite well organised. Because the cracks never showed: there always was food, miraculously it got cooked while you were out of the room, socks and shirts materialised, while you were shaving and changing your mind about your tie the children were transformed from pyjama'ed monsters into uniformed monsters with brushed hair and wiped faces and shoes and ready to go.

(b) Uniformed monsters

(a) Pyjama'ed monsters

. . . Transformed from pyjama'ed monsters into uniformed monsters

Is a new emotion creeping over you? Can it be, like a new dawn suffusing the eastern sky, a slow feeling of admiration for your wife and how she managed the household? Reluctant surprise at the realisation that the woman's lot is hard work? Especially if you have a family. Getting through it all takes time and, more important, it takes energy. Remember, you mustn't let the cracks show.

Think how pathetic the husband is who keeps bringing his kids to school late, or lets the neighbours find him eating bread and butter. You can do better than that.

So what are you going to do? You are going to *not let the job eat you up*. Don't let your best energies be taken by what you have to do. Don't get involved. Don't let the kids really annoy you. Pretend to be angry by all means. But remember to maintain that inner detachment.

Then you're on the way. All you've got to do now is get organised. And there is help on the horizon. Neighbours will help; you can get a cleaning lady, a window cleaner. Of course, they won't organise you. You have to organise them. But salvation is round the corner.

Salvation lieth in lists

> *Salvation consists*
> *In making lists.*
> *The devil desists*
> *Where list persists.*

This elaborate poetic motto tells you, in a word, the technique for getting organised: lists.

Inner preparation for writing a shopping list

Lists: it all comes back to you. You remember those bits of paper that used to lie around or fall out of your wife's shopping bag? They used to say things like:

Tuesday	Or:	*Wed*
~~sausages~~		~~ham~~
~~butter~~		~~marg~~
~~veg~~		~~fruit~~
~~chemist~~		~~cleaners~~

Yes, O friend, the items are crossed out. You must have eaten ham that day. What a good wife you had (or have).

Well, you can make lists too: *real* lists. And in this chapter we are going to provide you with some real lists: model lists. You can go straight out and use them. Recite them. Set them to music.

Fig. 1 Fussy list – wrong.

If you are a fussy devil you can make up an elaborate list such as the following.

Day of the week . . . Year . . . List no. . . .
                                        File copy: yes/no

Food items required (see Appendix A, Reference List 1)

    1.
    2.
    3. etc.

Non-food items (see Technical Appendix D for reminders of practically all commodities known to man)

    1. etc.

Emergency items (tourniquets, anti-snake-bite serum, etc.)

Classified reminder system:

    TODAY do I need any special –
    ● Nutritional perquisites?
    ● Articles of apparel?
    ● Hygienic perquisites?

A list like this is ridiculous and I would ignore it if I were you. In fact if I met anyone, male or female, using a list like that I would keep right away from their hygienic perquisites.

Now I come to think of it my wife did once keep a sort of Appendix A, Reference List 1 pinned to the back of a cupboard door. It was a list of common foods and kitchen substances. Not really a list of everything you could conceivably need. It was more modest than that. You were meant to glance at it and it would cause you to consider whether you needed to buy item X or item Y. It was in alphabetical order and began with apples. No, it began with anchovies. No, it began with tuna fish because tuna fish got missed out and was added later.

This list is (I think) still there but I never look at it. I stand in the middle of the kitchen and turn round slowly three times. Then I know where we need the extra power-point putting. I seize a piece of paper, spend five minutes looking for a pencil (or vice versa), and I write . . . I write . . .

I write List A.

List A is the classic, basic list. It always gets you out of trouble. If in doubt, buy List A. If you apply List A really rigorously and unremittingly for three months, it is theoretically possible for you to end up with 25 lb of butter in the fridge, but you will notice this when you can't get any more in.

This isn't a great problem because you then simply buy 5 cwt of mushrooms and use the butter to cook them.

Fig. 2   Useful lists – right. A, B and C.

List A – 'the classic, basic list'.

```
bread
butter
potatoes
onions
tuna fish
loo paper
```

List A is sublime in its simplicity. If it had seventeen syllables it would be a haiku.

Even List A can be boiled down further if you can get bread, butter and potatoes from the milkman. When you, or the rest of your family, are tired of List A you go on to more advanced lists. There are List B (Utility) and List C ('The Unfinished').

```
coffee              digestive bisc.
marg                satsumas
carrots             yog.
chicken?            sprouts
or chops?           toothpaste
PS eggs
PPS bacon
```

List B complements List A superbly in its compactness and its direct answer to life's challenge. List C immediately evokes that vision of the intimate late-night kitchen scene, as you casually but exquisitely perfect a little *bonne bouche* in your wok, while the loved one, or the desired one, waits and watches.

List C – 'The Unfinished'.

```
more onions         posh mayonnaise
avocado             organic rice
peppers             brown bread
leeks               saltless butter
pork fillet         froz. prawns
```

These of course are all food lists. We haven't touched upon the sensitive matter of booze. You don't make lists for booze. Your wife thinks you drink too much. You quietly buy it and shove it in the cupboard first when you get home.

Then, of course, there are the non-food lists. These are the documents that the man about the house can elevate to an art form. You sit down at the kitchen table in the morning. Your wife has gone to work. The kids have gone to school. The house is empty and quiet. You empty your mind.

Thoughts keep flitting back in like small clouds crossing the sky. You chase them out. They go pop! like bubbles and disappear.

After a while you begin to write. You write something like:

wash sheets
mend shirt
library books
gas bill

You pin it up on the notice board beside the other lists. You feel at peace. You are planning your day. Suddenly you jump up. You go and take the sheets off the bed. Beside the bed you find a library book. You go and round up the others while you think of it. Realising you haven't read them all, you think you'll have your coffee early and just have a quick look at one or two.

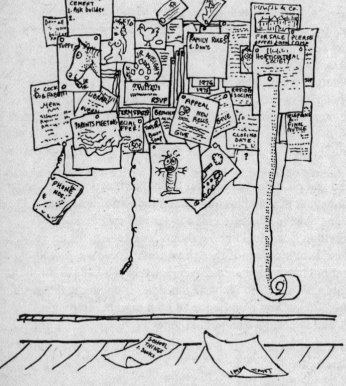

A useful layout for your kitchen noticeboard

Two hours later you look at your watch and remember you have to get to the shops before they shut for lunch. The day passes. That evening you find the sheets on the floor beside the bed. You put them back on it. A few days later you take down the accumulated lists and throw them away. You look in some drawers to find where you put the gas bill last reminder.

Planning – how it's really done

Real housewives make pukka schedules and know what they are supposed to be doing.

So that you can pretend you know what you are supposed, etc., we are providing two schedules. One is a weekly, one a daily schedule. See end of chapter.

You have to remember to alter the details of the schedule to fit your own timetable. Otherwise we would have the entire population of male housewives taking their kids to Brownies on the same night. What a droll idea. But excessive regimentation is bad for a nation of individualists. (That's what you think you are. You don't realise there are thousands like you, poor devils all.)

So you pin your schedule on the notice board. Each morning you look at it. Anything you pin on the notice board hides other things so you only ever have partial awareness of everything you should know about. You have to lift up your schedule to see when is the school parents' evening or end of term or church jumble sale. Alternatively you have to lift the jumble sale notice to see your schedule. It doesn't make much difference, as you rush past it all each morning reciting a kind of shouted poem which goes as follows.

verse 1 . . . Time?	*verse 2* . . . Time!
Where's my?	Hair!
Have you got your?	Shoes!
Why aren't you?	Keys!
Do I have to?	Money!
Oh God . . .	Oh God . . .

Poor God! He has nothing to do with your schedule and doesn't even make the notice covering it fall off.

So keep it up. Day after day. Laugh or cry, and hope the car will start. Remember, wives do it all the time. Perhaps they are different from us.

Nothing lasts for ever, you can remind yourself. Eventually the sun will blow up and engulf the planets.

Shopping – the essentials

The two principles of shopping are the following.

1 You can cash a cheque, or owe them till tomorrow, at the corner shop.
2 Walking round the supermarket saves making a shopping list.

Wives, or indeed women, think they know more about shopping than men. Like all silly theories, this is partly true. Examples:

★ Women inspect the little bags of carrots more carefully than men. True.
★ Men pack boxes at the check-out better than women. True.

Shopping is a pleasurable activity for many people because it is an escape. An escape from confinement or from chores into a bright world of lights, sounds and tempting objects. Our physical beings enjoy the stimuli of being out and about in shops. Our eyes and brains drink in the flow of reassuring impressions. Our financial beings may or may not enjoy paying the price at the end of the trip.

Transport, lifts and moral obligation

If you live in the middle of your village, or near a bus stop, or otherwise conveniently placed for shops, schools, friends and necessities, you are lucky.

If you don't, or if your family don't walk anywhere, or if you can't cross the road anyway because of the traffic, then you unfortunately need at least three, and preferably four cars, thus:

1 Wife's car.
2 Your car.
3 Spare car.
4 Spare spare car because the first three have all done 95,000 miles.

If you are normal and you only have one or one and a half cars, then you have to take your wife to the station on top of everything else. (Literally.) Or you can let Brian from No. 7 pick her up on his way. Perhaps you should get her a motorcycle.

If you have children, then you get involved in lifts. Lifts involve bringing your neighbours' children home from school. If they are girls they giggle together. If they are boys they re-read the *Beano* in silence. In the mornings practically everyone takes their own children because no one can face any unnecessary detours or greetings.

After a while you and your neighbours build up various debits and credits of moral obligation to each other. The first

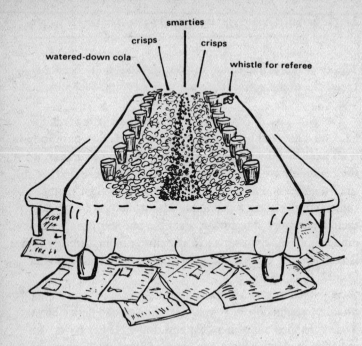

crisps

smarties

crisps

watered-down cola

whistle for referee

Table setting for inviting kids to tea

law of moral obligation to neighbours is that you resent debits
and credits equally, i.e. you resent your neighbour if she lets
you pick her kids up four times on the run and you also resent
your obligation if you let her pick yours up, etc.

Some people (nearly said 'some women') keep a tally and
know who owes whom how many lifts. The best thing to do is:

(a) when your kids are picked up manifest extreme gratitude
   and graciousness and force tiny presents on the other mum
   like a packet of biscuits or a cactus in a pot;

(b) have other kids to tea from time to time. Serve Coke and
   they will tell their mums they had a super time.

We will deal with certain moral matters, other than to do with
transport, pertaining to other wives and mothers in a delicate
chapter later on.

Planning your evenings with your wife

The crowning achievement of your day as a housekeeper is to spend the evening enjoying your wife's company. And she yours.

The puritans, or those who like to earn their rewards the hard way, say you have to plan for this, too. You have to have it all worked out so that when your wife gets home from work the children have had their supper and their baths and are in their nighties and all fragrant and drowsy for their mother to come and give them a goodnight kiss while you are reading them a last story. Meanwhile a simple but nourishing warm dinner is all ready to serve. In the sitting room a freshly lit fire is beginning to crackle and glow. Near it a modest red wine, uncorked, is warming.

As you come down from tucking up the children you glance proudly, yet modestly, at your schedule on the notice board. Your wife slips out of her coat and draws off her boots. Your eye rests momentarily on her rounded form. She intercepts your glance and a secret womanly smile touches her lips.

She sighs. 'What a lovely, welcoming house this is to come home to,' she murmurs. 'The children look well and so – so happy. And darling,' she adds, 'darling . . . you remembered to put the rubbish out.'

'Darling,' you declare, 'keeping the house nice for you is such a pleasure. And as for the rubbish – why, it was nothing. I only had to glance at my schedule. After all, it is Wednesday.'

'Your schedule?' she breathes. 'Tell me . . . what else is on your schedule?'

You catch your breath. Have you forgotten something? Evening class? The late-night chemist? Then you smile. The palms of your hands are moist. 'Darling,' you whisper. '*You* are.'

In the sitting room the fire flares hotly in the grate.

Fig. 3 – Your weekly timetable

Here is an example of somebody's actual working
timetable. Remember to alter the details to suit your family,
or you will turn up at Brownies on the wrong day.

Monday
8.45 Get children to school on time!!! Dinner money.
4.00 Collect Charlotte
4.30 Collect Charlie
5.30 Brownies
6.00 W. Cubs given up. Too old, thank heavens
6.45 Collect from Brownies
7.05 Dr Who

Tuesday
Charlotte recorder!! Babysitter!!
4.00 Collect Charlotte
4.30 Charlie stays to do prep!!
4.30 Charlotte music lesson
7.30 Furniture upholstery
7.30 Colloquial Arabic

Wednesday
Charlie football kit. Put out rubbish!!
4.00 Diana collects Charlotte
4.30 Collect Charlie *or* at 5.00 if away match
6.00 Collect Charlotte from Diana's

Thursday
Charlotte gym kit. Charlie piano lesson
12.30 Charlie piano
4.00 Collect Charlotte, Robin, Hazel, William, Lancelot &
Justin
4.30 Ann P. collecting Charlie
7.30 Residents' Association
7.30 Women's Institute

Friday
7.30 Charlie football kit + trainers. Extra milk Sat?
3.30 Charlotte early day
4.00 Charlie early day
Library

Saturday
10.30 Football practice
10.30 Riding lesson

Sunday
9.15 Church
6.00 Choir practice

Fig. 4 – Your daily timetable

Another actual timetable from recent experience to show you how to plan your day for maximum efficiency. The daily routine, of course, slots neatly into the overall weekly schedule.

7.15 Emerge from bed. Descend in dressing gown.

7.17 Let out dog who is anxious to chase paper-boy.

7.20 Wipe up dog shit. Shout and curse.

7.25 Put kettle on, make toast, etc.

7.30 Call family for breakfast. Chivvy children along lightly and good-humouredly, greet wife with gentle courtesy.

7.45 Retire to bathroom with newspaper.

7.46 Emerge, remind children about piano practice, homework, brush teeth, brush hair, brush shoes, be nice to each other, hurry up. Say goodbye to wife if she's leaving.

7.47 Retire to bathroom, etc.

8.15 Get car out. Take children to school. As they get out of car they remember various things urgently required, like a note for teacher, some money which you haven't got, their recorder which is at home, etc.

9.00 Return home, make coffee, read paper.

9.30 Ring up various mothers about who is collecting whom, whose children having tea with whom.

9.45 Go to shops, buy loaf of bread, pound of mince and a bottle of vodka.

10.30 Housework.

11.00 Coffee.

12.00 Go to office. Open letters. [If applicable.]

12.30 Lunch.

2.00 Call at cleaners. Buy vitamin pills at chemist. Take goldfish back to petshop.

2.30 Back to work. Read letters. [If applicable.]

3.30 Leave to start collecting children.

4.30 Home, make tea. Pour vodka into yours. Ignore children's accusing gaze.

5.30 Off to Brownies, piano practice or whatever.

6.30 Take other child to Wolf Cubs.

6.45 Collect first child from Brownies. You can't get there in time, of course. If you're lucky the other child is brought home by someone else.

7.30 onwards. Try to get children into bed. Remind them they have had their tea, lunch, etc. when they say they are still hungry. Give in and get the cornflakes out. Threaten them with no reading time. Remember they haven't done their homework.

Meanwhile . . . 6.30. Your wife gets home from work. Mix a gin and tonic. Bring her slippers. With another hand be devilling up a little surprise, like sauté kidneys, avocado fool, etc.

And if you're unstoppable . . . 7.30. Go to your evening class. Furniture upholstery or colloquial Arabic. Ask your wife if she minds babysitting. You may have a problem if your wife didn't come home this evening (sales meeting) or has gone to the pub with her girl friends.

2
Why do we bother?
or
Standards, status and infestations

IT MAY BE only when you have some responsibility for running
the household that you begin to reflect what kind of a family
you have. Families, after all, are tidy or untidy, serious or
merry – they have a sort of permanent corporate identity
regardless of how individuals are on their own or what happens
at particular moments.

In fact, the conspiracy theory applies to families – the
members of the family conspire together, usually
unconsciously, in the image they present and the standards
they accept.

Most of us try to project an image of ourselves which is an
extension of the self-image we like best and which we would
like the world to observe. We are all familiar with the problem
of how to react to the Joneses with their new car or their fur
coat or their sun tan. Why the Joneses act like that, and why
we act or react like this, is psychologically quite interesting –
but the subject of another book. If you are a husband in charge
of the house, just bear in mind that wives are socially more
sensitive than you about the home and what the home betrays
about the family. You might as well also remember that if you
persist in wearing jeans and sandals and driving an ancient
Morris Minor in order to look a bohemian, you risk being
considered by the other mothers (when you collect the
children) as not only (a) another kind of snob, but (b)
unreliable and (c) unattractive. They don't seem to notice
you're a bohemian, but then they don't pay much attention to
you anyway.

They don't seem to notice you're a bohemian

What Mother taught you

So why do you bother to keep the house up to scratch? Mostly, because your mother taught you to. Particularly if you were a boy, she doubtless didn't do much teaching as such.

But you grew up in her house and absorbed her example without realising it. Quite probably (it seemed to go with that generation) your parents were both keen on something called standards.

How boring it was, to be lectured on standards. Had you no standards? You had to have standards. How wonderful, to leave home as an adolescent or young adult, and get away from standards.

Then, mysteriously, later on, without you noticing, standards crept back in. Where did they come from? You find yourself telling your kids to eat properly, blow their noses, apologise to each other, and it isn't you speaking, it's standards. Or for some reason or other you are compelled to change the tablecloth, or air the sheets, or polish the doorknob. It isn't you, it's standards.

Mind you, standards do change. We don't seem to spring clean in the way that Mother did (and does). Perhaps we should. Also we don't seem to care about finding a spider behind the wardrobe in the way that Mother did (and does). I'm sure we're right about the spider.

But here you are. Your wife has gone to work. You're standing in the middle of the kitchen, holding the broom. And

you're remembering your mother. For a moment you *are* your mother, standing in her kitchen with her broom, thirty years ago or whenever it was. At the same time you are you as you were, half-size, seeing the room from below, feeling again that comfortable feeling of childhood we have mostly forgotten.

Occasionally you can make this connection with your
parents. All too often it only happens when one of them dies.
But it teaches you much about the continuity of human nature,
and about who you are, and why you are as you are. In fact
you are making a connection with another part of yourself. For
a moment you are in touch with something solid and
permanent in yourself – as distinct from the succession of
impulses and reactions which make up most of our daily
activity.

Image and reality

Talking of what is real and what isn't, how it is that we are
intimidated by the displays other people put on? When we go
to dinner and have to handle the host's silver and cut glass?
We *should* remain unmoved, accept things as they are, and be
amused but not amazed by the way people are . . .

Once we were invited to dinner by friends in Hampstead –
well, Golders Green. The conversation was of music and the
arts. As to the crockery – nothing matched. We all ate off
different-coloured plates of different sizes. We grasped various
kinds of knives and forks, some with pleasantly yellowed bone
handles. Afterwards we were amazed. We couldn't help it. We
admired the insouciance, the plain virtue, of the hostess. Why?
Why should we have reacted to the unposh as much as to the
posh? We should be more calm and consistent, and value only
the *real* – but human nature isn't like that.

And just as well too: what an endless source of amusement
we are to each other. After all, what purpose do we serve to
our neighbours other than to give them something to gossip
about, criticise or laugh at?

And now that you're a housewife (yes, you), you have to
recognise the signs and symbols. For example, when you come
to a break in the housework, and you pop over for a coffee
with your neighbour (does her husband know?), you notice her

vacuum cleaner standing in the hall. What does this mean?

An experienced reader of the signs, or a woman, will immediately know that this doesn't necessarily mean she has done any vacuuming, or is going to. Indeed, you may remember seeing it standing in another room when you were last in her house.

The vacuum cleaner standing about is intended to convey that she is conscientious about keeping her home clean and is in the process of doing so – whether she really is or not.

A more masculine version of this phenomenon entails keeping some repair or embellishment unfinished. You can

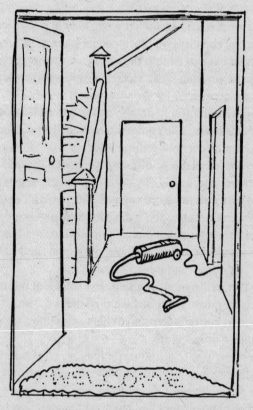

The vacuum cleaner as ornament

have a half-built extension around for quite a long time, and earn a great deal of praise and admiration for it, even though it is half-finished. You may need your wife on hand to point out that you are doing most of it yourself, as it would not be modest to say so yourself. You *can* say so yourself if visitors ask where the builders are on a Monday morning. If you are still pursuing the bohemian image you can say you ran out of money and they went away.

One of the most effective devices is to have the hall filled with scaffolding and planks and in a permanent state of being decorated. So everybody entering the house has to duck through the mess. You apologise. They marvel at the transformation. You know that what is incomplete is still full of infinite promise. In fact the conduct of your life is founded on that principle. You hope that while you are still alive you may get around to achieving at least one or two basic worthwhile things. Or at least one. You still imagine you're a promising teenager.

Bold spirits can develop the scaffolding syndrome into an art form and hold dinner parties amid dust-sheeted sideboards and the backs of furniture from other rooms.

They are saying to their neighbours: 'You can't classify us. Our status isn't defined. We're in transition. Perhaps you'll think our status will finish up higher than yours.'

But they are also saying: 'We refuse to compete on your terms. We're trying not to commit ourselves to a final state of décor in case our status becomes clear and you think it lower than yours.'

Some people genuinely don't care about material status and whether they are seen to be poorer than others. Their affectation is to appear superior in other respects.

Why you bother – the unsavoury reasons

Never mind the social and psychological reasons for maintaining your house in a particular way.

If you don't clean your house, sooner or later various physical, chemical and biological facts of life catch up with you. Not to mention the smell.

Cavemen knew this, but they either changed cave or brought in more earth and built the floor up. There are problems with these ancestral solutions.

In Figure 5, page 42 we give a detailed rating of the infestations you will surely get if you don't do the housework. And some you may already have. In the next section we offer some commentary on the most common conditions. This may even scare you, and so it should. Eventually there will come a point where neglect of basic household (and personal) hygiene has disagreeable consequences.

It's no good saying sages and gurus don't care about such things, their minds are on higher things. Gurus either have disciples who sweep up after them, or they live in air-conditioned hotels.

Some infestations you already have? Through no fault of your own? How unfair! But it's true. Even the best schools nowadays sometimes send apologetic notes home saying there has been a most unfortunate outbreak of – er – headlice and the application of Dermatismus has been found efficacious in most instances and could you please launder your child's towel and comb, and your child.

Again, if you have a cat, you almost certainly have cat fleas. Journalists write about cat fleas saying they are a middle-class condition so the middle class feel OK. People who know about cat fleas say they only live on cats, but people who don't know about cat fleas get bitten up to knee level. The fleas can't jump higher than this. But you get bitten above knee level as you lie in bed, assuming you allow your furry darling on the bed.

Helping your cat with its flea problem

Once when we lived in Finchley (yes, I know), we had a genteel cat-flea problem. In those days we were alarmed by such things and we rang the council, who sent round pest control officers. They said at the door, 'We've come about the – er – infestation.' They sprayed the floors and the walls up to knee height but not the cat, who had got out through his cat door.

When we moved to our house where the previous occupants had maintained a colony of twenty-seven/thirty-seven/forty-seven cats (estimates vary), we learned more. They (the human occupants, not the cats) were very charitable to strays, and soft-hearted, and obviously couldn't say no. Even so you don't just accumulate thirty-seven cats by doing nothing in particular. They must have been famous in the cat underworld. When we first visited, the windows were always open, we thought because it was summer. Our host, invited by his wife to rescue Fluffy from behind the sofa, would emerge dishevelled and bleeding while the lynx-like Fluffy streaked out of the window. Upstairs the character parts were in retirement, and under beds and on dressing tables you would find the somnolent shapes of Fred's Friend, One-Eye, No-Tail and Scratters.

What we learned from this menagerie was that cats and rats can coexist. The cats' food hung about and rotted, and the rats hung about and ate it. An extensive and pungent ecological system throve throughout and round about the house. When we arrived and stopped putting out scraps, the rats vanished too, with the exception of one or two defiant biggies which we had to trap. One had a body a foot long and its tail hung out over the side of the bucket. We heard the trap going off in the loft with a bang. Before that every night we listened to him doing press-ups over our heads as we lay in bed.

Infestations and afflictions

Herewith a brief commentary on the more common conditions which happen to the worst (and the best) households. Please write and tell us if you have a condition we have missed out.

Allergies. We all know people who get hay fever every year – perhaps you do. Or people whose eyes water when the cat jumps on their knee. Naturally the beast picks them out. But allergies are a serious and subtle matter – we're not just talking of your allergy to Mrs Pauncefoot which induces a strange sense of physical constriction whenever she enters the room you are in. Keep the dust and fur levels in your house down – vacuum in the corners.

Athlete's foot. Also known as foot rot. Caused by a fungus. Can be hard to eradicate – once you've had it, it can break out again in favourable conditions. Caught in changing rooms, not necessarily your fault at source, but fostered (or festered) by hot, sweaty unwashed feet and socks. Best course: keep feet dry with powder. Not sexy.

Bedbugs. You have to be pretty dirty to get bedbugs. Bedbugs sound vaguely old-fashioned. They conjure up pictures of seedy hostels. In fact anyone who has stayed in cheap hotels in various exotic parts of the world will have encountered the odd bug. For those who don't know, bedbugs are flat ill-smelling blood-sucking insects. They bite you at night.

Beetles. Beetles tend to saunter in through the back door, especially if you live in the country. In most respects they are strictly neutral, i.e. they don't leave a mess, they don't smell and they don't make much noise. It's no good bringing the dog to eat one like when you have dropped a piece of butter. The dog will only sniff a beetle. You can spend many happy moments on hands and knees flicking the beetle back towards the door. After twenty minutes you tread on it by mistake. 'Oops! Sorry, beetle,' you say, hoping it won't count against you. The famous story by Kafka called *Metamorphosis* is about waking up transformed into one.

Blocked drains. Can be caused by:

(a) a fallen tree;
(b) using newspaper instead of lavatory paper;
(c) a dead rat.

You should be able to tell if either of the first two factors is responsible. If you really get a blocked drain you can telephone a service with a name like Klere-Drane and they come along and poke the rat or whatever it is out of the way with rods. What usually happens is that they lift the lid of the inspection chamber and you are all standing round looking into it when something unmentionable floats into view.

We once had a smell in the house for a few days. It wafted about a bit and my wife explained to visitors that a mouse must have died under the sink. In fact we had had a new sink fitted and with true diagnostic wizardry I realised the plumber had forgotten to put in a trap. A trap is the little downward loop of pipe under the sink which stays full of water and the water stops the smell coming back up from the drains. Very clever.

Cockroaches. If you have bedbugs in the bed, you are quite likely to have cockroaches under it. Cockroaches seem nicer than bedbugs, but this is probably only because they don't get into bed with you. They tend to infest kitchens and come out at night. Again, if you have ever stayed in a cheap hotel and come in late, you might have seen dozens of them scuttling for the skirting when you turned the light on. For added nostalgia you might have crunched one underfoot on the stairs.

Crabs. Crabs, apart from on the sea shore, are small lice which infest the pubic region. You can tell if you have them because you itch and you also find tiny bloodstains on your underpants (or knickers) from ones that have got squashed. You usually get them from sexual congress (wonderful expression) with someone who has 'em, but you can get them from towels if you're unlucky or daft.

Crabs are quite good value conversationally because of the associated sexual *frisson*. Crabs are considered jokey and it is OK to have a certain knowledge of them. This suggests that you are a person of the world, and that you were sexually active (another good expression) in your past, even if not now. Treatment for crabs usually consists of shaking medicated powder down the front of your pants.

Damp rot. Less common, and more interesting, than dry rot, but more blame attaches to damp rot. You are expected to mend a leaking gutter or tackle rising damp, before part of your floor or wall becomes gungified.

Dry rot. Dry rot is OK because practically everybody living in an oldish house has it. Also you can get it treated so you don't feel too threatened. If it goes too far, then you have to get it cut out and the timberwork replaced. Dry rot is actually the decay of unventilated timber caused by various fungi. The timber becomes light and crumbly.

Ingrowing toenails are usually your own fault unless you can't bend down that far.

Lice. 'Real' lice infest the body, generally feeding on the host's blood and transmitting disease. Typhus is transmitted by lice in some parts of the world.

If you are a harmless and only moderately inefficient housekeeper, your problem may be merely with the headlouse.

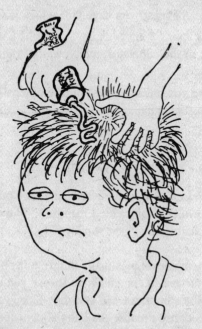

Helping your children with their headlice problem

Your kids pick up headlice at school – this is when you get strangely worded notes from the school secretary and you rush to the chemists to buy various ultra-expensive shampoos. Meanwhile you are driven mad by the kids scratching their heads. Headlice seem to come and go in cycles or perhaps (for the lice) fashions.

Mice. If you like small furry creatures then mice are quite, so to speak, nice. It can be a nuisance finding mouse droppings in your kitchen drawers, but mice generally have quite a favourable image. Mice are useful in conversation, and even more so if a mouse actually appears in the room, as the topic enables men and women to grasp each other for reassurance. In theory cats catch mice.

Mildew. You find mildew, or mould, on damp things. You can find it on any of the following:

★ the only piece of bread you have left, which was all right yesterday;

★ a pot of jam in the cupboard, which was all right three weeks ago;

★ a pan of soup you meant to heat up the other day;

★ a piece of cheese which rolled under the cupboard heaven knows when;

★ a box of apples you were keeping under the stairs which you have put your hand into in the dark.

You can also find mildew in cupboards and on clothes and bedding and down the wall behind furniture. The answer is to keep the place ventilated. Open windows.

Nappy rash. Most people eventually outgrow nappy rash – even the baby survives it somehow. In theory you are supposed to keep your baby's bottom clean and dry. Since you fail regularly in this partly because the baby always does it as soon

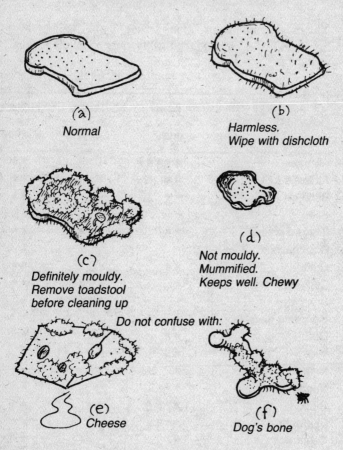

Spotting a mouldy piece of bread

(a)
Normal

(b)
Harmless.
Wipe with dishcloth

(c)
Definitely mouldy.
Remove toadstool
before cleaning up

(d)
Not mouldy.
Mummified.
Keeps well. Chewy

Do not confuse with:

(e)
Cheese

(f)
Dog's bone

as you have put a clean nappy on, you have to keep a large tube of a certain wonder pink cream handy.

Nits. Nits are the young of headlice. They cling to hairs or to the scalp. You could be forgiven for thinking, when you raise the subject at a coffee morning, that nobody else's children has them. Then you realise they whisper about them. In some areas in the old days a nit nurse used to come around.

Figure 5 – Infestations and afflictions, with star rating

The most common conditions arising if you don't keep your house and its occupants reasonably clean. The more stars, the worse.

Condition	Threat to health	Threat to building	Quick to come
Allergies	★★★★★	–	★★★★★
Athlete's foot	★★	★	★★
Bedbugs	★★	–	★★
Beetles	–	–	–
Blocked drains	★★	★★★	★★★
Cockroaches	★	★	★
Crabs	★★	–	★★
Damp rot	★	★★★★	★★
Dry rot	–	★★★★★	★
Ingrowing toenails	★	–	★
Lice	★★	–	★★
Mice	★	–	★
Mildew	★	★	★
Nappy rash	★★	–	★★★★
Rats	★★★★	★★	★★
Ringworm	★★	–	★★
Roundworm	★	–	★★★
Silverfish	★	★	★
Smelly house	★	★	★★
Smelly people	★★★	–	★★
Spots	★★	–	★★★
Threadworm	★★★★	–	★★
Woodlice	–	★	★

Slow to go	Your fault	Smelliness	Horror rating	Conversational value
★★★★★	★★★	★	★★	★★★
★★★	★★★★★	★★	★★★	★
★	★★★★	★★★	★★★★	★★
–	–	–	–	★
★	★★★	★★★★★	★★	★★★
★	★	★	★	★
★★★	★★★	★	★★	★★★★
★★★★	★	★	★	★★
★★★★★	–	★	–	★
★	★★★	★	★★	★
★★	★★	–	★★★	★★★
★★	★	★★	★	★★★
★★	★★	★★	★	★
★★	★★★★★	–	★	★
★★★	★★★★	★★★★★	★★★★★	★★★★★
★★	★★★	–	★★	★★
★★★	★	–	★★★	★
★★	★★★★	–	★★★	★
★★★★★	★★★★★	★★★★★	★★★	★★★
★	★★★★★	★★★★★	★★★★	★★★
★★★	★★★★	★	★★	★
★★★★	★★★	–	★★★	★
★★	★★	–	★★★	★★

Rats. Rats are the winners, practically in all departments – just look at their performance in the star rating table. They even get stars for threatening the structure of the house, as anyone will confirm who has seen the bottom of doorposts gnawed through.

Rats are no longer carriers of the bubonic plague – not in this country at any rate – but they remain potential carriers of disease and the arch-symbol of the pestiferous. Above all, they stink. They have a rather wonderful stink. If you have rats in your loft you will find they make cosy nests of chewed-up old love letters between the joists. Then the love letters stink. The draughts coming from chinks in the skirting and floorboards stink too. As you pull out the nest in gloved hands – it makes two bucketfuls – fragments of your or someone else's love life flutter before your eyes: 'Dearest George . . . the tennis party was . . . I am sorry that Freddie . . . before we change our minds . . .' all embalmed in the robust fragrance of the rat.

Talking of the plague, one of the half-timbered houses in the old city of Chester is called God's Providence House, because the inhabitants were spared the plague in the seventeenth century. The building was supposedly used to store onions and garlic. Either the occupants ate their own stores and stayed uncommonly healthy, or the garlic kept the rats away.

Rats definitely arouse in us an age-old aversion. We must have folk memories of rats scampering over us while we sleep and nibbling at the baby. Rats have the No. 1 horror rating and evoke the strongest shock reaction in conversations with neighbours.

After all, if you have rats, your neighbour has them too. In bygone days people tended to live closer to their own rubbish and generally speaking where there is refuse, there are rats. Try taking your old mattress to the local dump on a quiet evening or very early in the morning, and sit and wait.

So if you want rats, just leave rubbish around the place, and sit and wait.

Ringworm. Not a worm but a contagious disease of the skin or hair, caused by fungi characterised by ring-shaped patches. Kids get it from each other. Not entirely your fault, but the neighbours think you're unsavoury. Even when their kids get it they still think you're unsavoury because yours gave it to theirs.

Roundworm. 'There are very few animals that don't have them in one form or another,' says the doctor's leaflet reassuringly and threateningly at the same time. Similar to threadworm.

Silverfish. Small silvery insect which turns up in dank and musty carpets and corners and darts about.

Smells. Smells rate quite well in the rating table – assuming it isn't you who have the problem. Perhaps as more men stay at home and join in the ladies' coffee mornings, the present lamentable reticence about this subject will diminish.

Some smells are OK, e.g. cooking with garlic smells. French cigarette smells are OK if you like French cigarette smells. Cabbagy cooking smells are not OK. The truly disagreeable smells come from all the awful things discussed previously, i.e. broadly speaking from dirt – particularly organic dirt, we add with relish.

Solution to smells: clean up. Air the house. What a lovely expression. Air the house. You do it by opening windows.

You can always go around spraying an aerosol air freshener entitled Fern or Sandalwood (perhaps it should be Bogwort or Bladderwrack). But this is like the old Elizabethans walking around wearing a perfumed pomander and never taking a bath.

Spots. You get spots either by being an adolescent or by having too much syrup on your butties. Eat plenty of fresh fruit, your mother would say.

Staring eyes. This is not an infestation but a condition to watch out for in your neighbours. If they have it when visiting you, ask politely what the cause is.

(a)
Something in the hall

(b)
Something in the lavatory

(c)
Something in the dinner

If neighbours have staring eyes when they visit you, it may be something in your house.

(d)

Something on you

Tape worm. Serious and debilitating. Not worth having.

Threadworm. This is a very merry condition, which all the family can share. The dog has 'em, the cat has 'em, the children have 'em and if you're not careful you get 'em.

A doctor writes: The condition is marked by anal itching, particularly at night. (The worms come out and wander around.) A doctor continues after that interruption: Slender white thread-like worms may sometimes be discerned in the stools. (Doctors always say stools.) So we say to the kids: Don't flush the loo, I want to have a look, etc. This is what being a parent means.

The trouble is that the children touch the animals, or they scratch their itchy bums in the night, and then they put their fingers back in their mouths, and round it goes.

You can buy worm medicine for both humans and animals. But at different shops.

Woodlice. Repulsive but friendly and good natured. They like damp woodwork and bricks. Friends in Wiltshire had them in the loo and in the teapot.

Common sense and the bottle of bleach

Matter-of-fact people, including experienced housewives, tend to say:

'Nonsense! Things don't go that far. So what if a bit of dirt piles up? You don't suddenly start getting smells and rats and diseases.'

This school of thought tends to favour the bottle of bleach technique. Thus:

'I find, if things have gone a bit far, a bottle of bleach works wonders. Pour it into the loo/down the sink. Have a good scrub round with it.'

This rather dashing approach should appeal to the man about the house who has let the filth creep up on him. But you can't pour bleach over the children. For that matter you can't pour it over the furniture or over your clothes.

So what do you do? You use your common sense! If you live in a hot country, or in summer, things go off quickly. On the other hand, when it's chilly, things stay damp.

We would put discretion before desperation. The wise man cleans his house today, and keeps tomorrow's bugs away.

3
Housework
or
Stopping the filth from being apparent

REAL HOUSEWIVES know that housework is a combination of
what you have time for and what you have to do so things
don't look absolutely awful.

Some homes, where the wife works and the husband
pretends he has an important job, get into a permanent state of
reinforced mess which can be quite attractive. This is a state in
which the edges of all the rooms are piled with boxes and
newspapers and children's clothes and toys, and the living

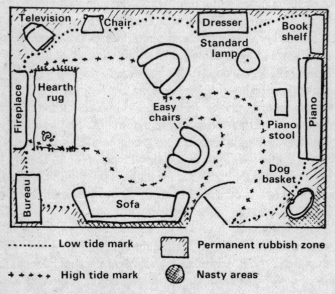

Television   Chair   Dresser   Book shelf
                       Standard lamp
Fireplace Hearth rug   Easy chairs   Piano
                        Piano stool
                        Dog basket
Bureau   Sofa

·········· Low tide mark   Permanent rubbish zone

+ + + + + High tide mark   Nasty areas

Diagram of sitting room showing layout of mess

space in the middle gets steadily smaller. If your house is in this state, then take advantage of it by ensuring that the space in the centre of each room is roughly circular and therefore easier to vacuum in a few seconds.

Another benefit of the RM (reinforced mess) syndrome is that it attracts an agreeable and relaxed category of visitor who enjoys sitting marooned in an easy chair behind the cat litter and the pile of darning. You can have good talks about life, death and the advantages of marriage with a visitor like this, who will oblige you by leaving his (or her) pipe and beer glass on the floor beside the chair. This helps to cement the RM together.

The opposite of the RM is the CT (compulsive tidiness) state. This is unlikely to be your problem. It can usually only be observed in the houses of women who are at home most if not all of the time, and who were rigorously potty-trained by their mothers. Or fathers. Not that you – or indeed they – would know this. The CT phenomenon is distinctly uncanny and menacing. We had a terribly charming and attractive friend, with two small boys, who exhibited this syndrome. If you visited her unexpectedly at ten o'clock in the morning, she would be standing amiably and fragrantly in the middle of spotless hall. You would rush past her into the kitchen – nothing: no breakfast dishes, no toast crumbs, yards of perfectly empty working surface, the cupboards closed. Then rush into the sitting room – same: no toys, no half-finished things lying around. Even the kids' bedroom – beds made, pyjamas folded. Where was it all, you wondered? In the cupboards? Did they all do it, or did just she do it? I wanted to open a kitchen cupboard in the hope that a vast jumble would fall out on me, like in a cartoon.

The CT woman can evoke, in the male observer, a certain sexual curiosity – but that is the subject of another book. Fortunately, the RM woman can also evoke sexual curiosity in male observers, and that should at least be the subject of another chapter

There is also a household state known as the happy medium, where things are quite tidy, quite clean, quite organised, etc. There is not much point in aiming at this state since you will tend to finish up in it anyway. You have to be determined, energetic and consistent to have either a very tidy or a very untidy house. Most of us secretly admire extremes because they are more interesting but fall in the middle ourselves. This applies to politics, sex, motoring and conversation at parties as well as housework.

Cultivating the right attitude

You have to care enough, but not too much, about housework. This principle applies to most things in life. When you button your shirt, use enough energy but not too much. When you run the vacuum cleaner, get the carpet clean, but don't take it too seriously.

You use what energy you want to use. Housework is a good opportunity for exercise if you are keen on exercise. Curiously, some religious sects prescribe violent exercise for their adherents with the idea that it enables them to relax more fully afterwards. Of course, if you have to go off in the afternoon or evening and dance or sing or play football, you should guard against letting the dusting exhaust you.

You can do housework well enough if first of all you think about it in the right way. You have a certain amount of time available, certain things may have to be done, there may be conflicts of priorities, you may not want to do any anyway. So you accept all that. You see that all those considerations are going on inside you. You see that you are grappling with:

(a) your own expectations;
(b) your idea of someone else's expectations, e.g. your wife's, your mother's, The Great Housekeeper in the Sky's;

(c) a vague idea of the objective state of the house and the effect on it your work will have.

In these circumstances you cry, 'Balls to expectations!' and proceed to do whatever is reasonable. You may decide to do either:

(a) as much as possible; or
(b) some or a bit; or
(c) none.

The important thing to remember is that it doesn't matter what you do as long as your reasons are logical and you don't kid yourself.

Not kidding yourself has to do with trying to recognise what is really going on and accepting the consequences. It's another counsel of perfection, since most of the time we kid ourselves to a greater or lesser extent. But you come to see when other people are kidding themselves and don't know it. You can observe the elaborate pretences people erect.

It is vital (as you open the broom cupboard) not to make yourself the victim of imagined expectations. Don't be a martyr. You can see people being martyrs everywhere. They think they're earning points. Most of the time they are accumulating anger and resentment, normally repressed. All sorts of terrible consequences can ensue from repressed anger – but that is the subject of another book.

Priorities

We need to get down to some practical detail.

Your wife has left for work. You have got back home after taking the kids to school. You are going to your office, or wherever, later. So where do you start?

At this stage, you can privately acknowledge that women

don't do badly to keep the house habitable and presentable, especially when they have other things to do as well. If you don't acknowledge it now, you will after a week or a month.

You start with the breakfast things. You either wash them up or put them in the dishwasher. You clear the table and wipe it. You give the bits of toast to the dog, refraining from kicking it (see chapter on pets). You sweep the floor. You try to shut the cupboard doors, open them, jam the jam in further and jam them shut again.

Then you run upstairs.

You run upstairs not because you are desperate for a pee, although this depends how many cups of tea you have already drunk. You run upstairs because you are observing the first principle of housework. You run or, if your house is cramped, you trot about your work. You have run upstairs to make the beds.

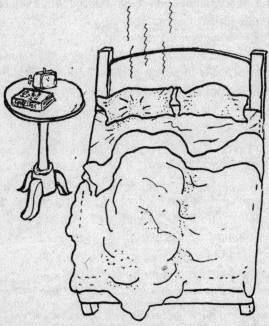

Don't make the bed if you can keep a cocoon going

How to make a bed

1 Enter bedroom. Locate bed. Draw curtains.

2 Sit on bed, read yesterday's newspaper.

3 Remember mission, jump up, address bed.

4 Shove bed back up to wall at head.

5 Fold back covers and contemplate vista of wrinkles, stains, crumbs, etc.

6 Hurl pillows off on to floor.

7 Proceed from corner to corner of bed, trying to get wrinkles out of bottom sheet.

8 Go round bed several times doing this.

9 Observe wryly that you can't get rid of last wrinkle.

10 Sweep crumbs, etc., off sheet.

11 Pull up top sheet.

12 Find everything is untucked at bottom of bed.

13 Make bottom of bed.

14 Pull up bedclothes, try not to have one side trailing on floor.

15 Tuck in nicely all round, muttering, 'So much for hospital corners.'

16 Put pillows back, plumping them up because you've seen other people do it. This is done by punching them playfully.

17 Carefully spread eiderdown, crocheted bedspread, etc.

18 Get into bed and read newspaper.

Note 1 If you have a continental quilt, replace Nos 11–17 with: Shake quilt so stuffing comes to your side, replace on bed.
Note 2 If you live in Switzerland, hang bedclothes over windowsill. The crumbs will fall out for the birds.

How you actually make a bed is the subject of another book; or for a quick guide you can consult technical checklist No. 1. If your wife is not coming home tonight, or indeed for several nights, there is much to be said for not making the bed. Not only does this save time and psychic energy. It also perpetuates a pleasant, perfectly formed cosy cocoon, assuming you get out of bed carefully in the morning.

Strictly speaking, of course, before you run or trot anywhere you have made a list of *priorities*. Housewives sometimes do this. Your wife may or may not be the sort of person who does. You are supposed to sit down and make a plan. A list of priorities may look like this:

1 Breakfast things.
2 Beds.
3 Spare bedroom.
4 Socks!
5 Hairdresser.
6 Priscilla.

You may feel that not all of the above applies to you, or not this morning at any rate. On the other hand it makes quite a good general-purpose priority list as long as you remember to change No. 6 from time to time.

In our house we have had quite a good list of priorities pinned to a bookcase for several years. It is not entirely relevant as it deals with much greater issues than breakfast and socks, but it has a strangely reassuring quality and also demonstrates eternal principles about lists of priorities.

★ Move rubble/sort bricks.
★ Floor in bathroom.
★ Garage roof.
★ Tidy potatoes.
★ Remove dead plumbing.
★ Sitting-room fireplace.
★ Clip hedge.

★ Transplant beeches.
★ Clean out summer house.
★ Remove dead list.

Seven years and more after we moved house I still look affectionately at this list as it hangs, faded and curling, in the study. The last item was added in another hand after a year or two. One may marvel at how things either get done or don't get done and time passes anyway.

Meanwhile you are sitting at the kitchen table thinking about your list of priorities.

Thinking about your list of priorities

If you can't begin it's probably because you are reflecting that a number of priorities is a logical impossibility. A priority is something you do before something else. If you have several priorities you can't do them all before each other. This is very consoling.

Perhaps if you put them in a list and number them this means that some priorities are more prior than others. If you suffer from genuine linguistic anguish in this way you have to call your list 'things to do'. You number the things on it in order to prioritise them.

As you sit, thinking your way through this set of impediments to action, why not go the whole hog and decide positively *not* to make a list of priorities? You can justify this philosophically too. You know that things are always waiting there to be done, that you are a mere pawn of external circumstances and geographical accident, that whatever you do makes a little difference but not much, so you may as well just bumble through.

Unfortunately this isn't quite good enough. You are supposed to be taking your responsibilities semi-seriously. So you have to recognise the pattern – and the pattern is as follows:

1 Basic things have to be done every day, or the house quickly becomes a total mess.
2 Other things have to be done at regular intervals, or the house gradually becomes a total mess.

Basic things include:

★ Dishes.
★ Beds.
★ Tidying.

You have done these except the tidying, and how much tidying you do depends on how tidy you are. Other things include:

★ Bathroom and lavatory.
★ Vacuuming.
★ Dusting.
★ Polishing.
★ Windows.

So, there you are. Today you're going to do basic things plus one or two other things. That sounds much better than a list of priorities. You just wait.

Tidying

Tidying is a rather relative thing. Einstein probably formulated the theory of relativity not when travelling on a tram in Zürich but when tidying his room. He obviously knew that the position of random objects lying about in a room is affected by the position of the observer and vice versa. This is why if you really want something you can't find it, and if you can't find it you get mad.

If you suffer from CT (compulsive tidiness – see earlier in chapter), then you have to have everything perfectly tidy: everything put away; nothing showing. This state really shows that you have a strong desire to be dead, when your life has been tidied away once and for all. No loose ends, nothing sticking out – static.

In most houses, however, life goes on, and human and animal activity produces a continuous redistribution of objects round the house. If you could take one of those films where the shutter clicks once an hour and then run it at normal speed, you would see a ghostly hail of slippers, books, glasses, toys, apple cores, coins, scraps of paper, some changing place, some moving further and further, some materialising, some rolling out of sight, some being overlaid by fresh detritus.

What do you do about it? Despair? Ignore it? First, you consider it. This helps you accept your family's mess level. Each family has a fairly consistent level of tidiness or untidiness, more or less regardless of how much you do about it individually – unless you work yourself to the bone – because there is a communal acceptance by the family of the state they are comfortable with. So do a bit of tidying. Don't go mad. Keep one or two particular places tidy. And look after your things. The others can look after their own: you're not their slave. Are you?

The bathroom and lavatory

Wives are very finicky about the bathroom and lavatory. So if you are pretending to be a housewife, you have to pretend to be finicky too. When your wife gets home in the evening and is trying to relax over a gin and tonic, you say to her, 'I cleaned the bathroom *thoroughly* today, dear. Will you *please* try not to get it so steamed up/spill talcum powder everywhere/splash so much water out of the bidet?' She won't love you more for this but it shows you are a force in the household.

The simplest way to clean the bathroom and lavatory is to concentrate on the handbasin. Remove the tidemark, mop out all the soapy gunge and wipe the drips and splashes. You can use the face flannel for all this as long as you rinse it and squeeze it out afterwards.

A clean and dry handbasin is quite impressive and you should contrive for your wife to be the first to wash her hands and splash it.

If you are inclined to do more in the B&L you can attempt any of the following. (Sounds like an exam paper: 'Attempt any three of the following. Give reasons.')

★ Clean bath with cleansing paste or pan-scrubber.
★ Wipe mirror.
★ Change towels.
★ Vacuum up fluff, talc, etc.
★ Straighten toothpaste tube.
★ Clean lavatory.

If you live in a hard-water area the last of these is a horrific job as the lavatory pan below the water level gradually and remorselessly gets coated with scale; like the inside of the kettle; doubtless like your inside too. One course is to kneel in front of the lavatory (reminds you of puking in your youth) and scrub it with Vim. Another course is to buy a new lavatory. When we moved into our house I removed some of the scale with a chisel. Later we bought a new one (and a new chisel). You could also install a water softener but they are not cheap. Or you could move house to a soft-water area. Or you could put a colouring tablet in the cistern so the bowl is filled with pretty blue or orange water.

Vacuuming

The hardest part about vacuuming is getting the vacuum out of the cupboard. This problem is nothing to do with the cupboard, it is known as moral inertia. Once the vacuum is out the rest is quite simple. Sometimes you notice that your wife has got it out and left it ready for you.

These events are related to the fact that it is easy to do either the preparation for a task or the task itself, but not as easy to

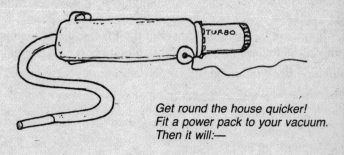

Get round the house quicker!
Fit a power pack to your vacuum.
Then it will:—

— weed garden

— remove nits

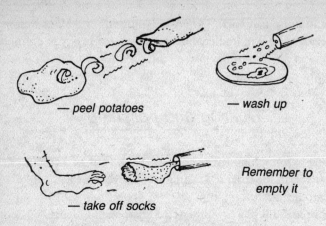

— peel potatoes

— wash up

— take off socks

Remember to empty it

Advanced techniques with the vacuum cleaner

do both in succession. A well-known example of this is running out of lavatory paper. How we hate to sit down and find there is no loo paper left. So next time if we notice it is running low, we get another roll from the cupboard. But we leave it for the next person to fit on the wall.

Vacuuming is something men can feel OK about since it involves machinery. With ingenuity you could fit extra wheels and an outboard and ride about on the back of your vacuum, or modify the lawn mower. You could also boost the suction power of your vacuum to get round the house quicker but you'd have to be careful what you pointed it at.

If you haven't much time, just vacuum your bedroom. This earns appreciation and may be worth a backscratch, depending on the currency of your household. However, there is extra merit in vacuuming the stairs. This is more agreeable than you would expect, partly because the job is neatly fragmented and also because of the clumping of the vacuum over the steps.

You usually can't vacuum the kids' room because you suck up marbles, sweet papers and pyjama legs.

If your pets are moulting you can try vacuuming them but if they don't like it you're not supposed to persist. Incidentally, when you vacuum you should move the furniture, vacuum under it and put it back. Otherwise your wife will think you're not serious and will lose confidence in other things you do or pretend to do.

Dusting and polishing

Dusting is something left over from the days of housemaids and Victorian nicknacks. Dusting is what you used to help your mother with.

There are still places you have to dust, such as ledges under tables and the piano. Pianos have a particular affinity with dust. Dusting has a certain importance because dust and what it contains provoke allergic reactions in some people.

If you have nothing else to do you can gather all the dusters together and wash them in the washing machine. This is a rather esoteric activity which most men don't know is ever done.

Polishing is hard work but pleasant on account of the smell of the polish, assuming you are polishing wood and not tiles. And the sight of a well-polished table or floor brings a glow of emotion even to the hardened breast. You are becoming house-proud.

You can buy, hire or borrow floor polishers, which are fine for a lot of floor but tricky on coffee tables.

Polishing the silver

You mean you haven't been burgled yet? Don't polish your silver. Take it to the bank.

Windows

Don't clean the windows. If it is sunny you can say, 'Doesn't the sun show up *every* speck of dust on those windows!'

If it is raining you can say, 'Doesn't it *always* rain just after I have cleaned the windows!'

If it is dull you say nothing. You hire a window cleaner.

4
Washing, ironing & mending
or
Cleanliness is next to low cunning

YOU'RE NOT really afraid of the washing? Surely a grown man can deal with a pile of laundry. You're quite good at other things.

You even think you're the expert in some areas – mechanical matters, for example; the car; wiring things; mending things. And then you're strong. You do the heavy jobs. You can carry bricks and logs.

How odd that your wife not only humps piles of washing around but knows how to work the machine. For that matter she moves the piano to clean behind it, or at least to get pencils out, but you don't know about this.

Men definitely have a blind spot where some household machines are concerned. They refuse to learn. There is a sort of unwillingness to be involved and to pay attention.

It's not really all that difficult. Nowadays there are even instructions printed on the front of the washing machine. On the opposite page we are happy to offer illustrations of the new International Code of washing machine symbols. These symbols make it perfectly clear what is going on. They are very new and you may not find them on all the machines currently in the shops.

For all the supposed easiness of doing the wash, wives have all kinds of horror stories about their husbands when faced with the reality of dirty laundry.

Part I – The new International Code

How lucky we are that a standard international set of symbols has been evolved painstakingly by British manufacturers' associations, trans-European consumer groups, pan-American academy design committees, and is now available on all Japanese-made washing machines

Heavy soil. No. 1 wash. Full spin

Medium soil. No. 2 wash. Full spin

Light soil. No. 3 wash. Half spin

Whites. No. 4 wash. Not sure how much spin

Fast coloureds. Overdrive. Give 'em a whirl

Non-fast coloureds. No. 27 wash. Rotate slowly

Woollies. No. 6 wash. Half spin

Delicates. No. 7 wash. Tiny spin

Specials. Wipe by hand. Full spin

Part II – Optional extras

Leave things to stew. Stir once a day

Washes football boots. Half spin

Special sock wash. Add fumigant pellets

Washes your pet. Wash as for woollens. Half spin

Take goldfish out before putting wash in

Special non-iron wash. Leaves everything crumpled and knotted

Don't put the washing in. This is the television set

Potato programme. Peels and cooks up to 7 lb potatoes

Machine's bust. Wash 'em in the bath

The new International Code of washing machine symbols

One woman said, 'When I had my babies I tried to go into hospital for only two days. When I got home there wasn't a made bed in sight and poor Ted, bless his heart, had tried to run a wash and put the woollies and blouses in with a track suit and everything, but everything, came out frizzy and blue.'

A story like this is absurd and pathetic. It leads us to formulate the first two principles of laundry for men:

1 Go to the laundrette if you like. You may like the company even if you've nothing to wash.
2 If you do go to the laundrette, don't take anybody's clothes except your own and maybe the dog's blanket.

But you'll feel differently about doing the wash after reading this chapter. We're going to give you technical knowledge *and* confidence. What a winning combination! Like Rubinstein at the piano. Mind you, you should have seen him at the washing machine.

Technical knowledge

This will inevitably be a long, complex section. Technical knowledge entails acquiring the following skills.

1 Turning the dial. If a No. 3 wash is required turn the dial to No. 3. If necessary put the aerial up to get better reception.
2 Opening the washer. Turn the machine off before opening the door, otherwise gallons of water will leap forth and pour all over the floor. This is bound to happen to you several times anyway, so practise chuckling to yourself and humming while you mop it up. While you're at it remove the mould growing on the floor under the washer from the leak you had mended again last week.
3 Full spin *v.* half spin. Resist the temptation to set everything to full spin so it gets drier quicker. You don't want your lacy nothings damaged, do you? And half spin leaves things

nicely damp for ironing, doesn't it? But full spin is the correct setting for lettuce.

Sorting the dirty clothes

This is where it really begins. Technical knowledge – fine: you can be a whizz with the settings. You can even learn to open the door by accident and shut it again quickly before the water comes out. But technical wizardry is as naught if you haven't got what it takes to sort dirty clothes ready for the wash.

For this, O friend, is where the wash *really* gets done. This is the planning stage. Planning, yes, foresight, intuition, imagination, experience, flair – they all come together here. And a sense of smell.

If you can really sort dirty washing you can be, not necessarily a great one, but a very good housekeeper indeed.

To sort washing you need a lot of space.

Sorting the washing entails making a lot of different piles of clothes. As a general rule, the more piles the better. It shows you are very sensitive to achieving the perfect wash for each garment. Piles of washing can also be left around on the floor and if any visitor dares venture upstairs she (of course) will see you are in the middle of a wash and what's more some of the sorting is absolutely brilliant. Of course, a lot of little washes use more water and your ecological sensitivity may oblige you to jam a few pairs of socks in together.

We now offer specific and practical guidelines for sorting the laundry by giving what is known as the standard piles listing (or SPILL) of dirty washing (or DW). This list has a certain beauty. It will excite the ardour of the Widow Twanky dormant in many of you.

1 Socks – woolly.
2 Socks – nylon.
3 Socks – indeterminate.

4 Smalls.

5 Bigs.

6 Jeans.

7 Jean's.

8 Hankies – white.

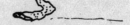

Your son's washing

9 Hankies – revolting.

10 Bras and knickers.

11 Knickers and bras.

12 Cotton knickers (all right. Get on with it).

13 Filthy old overalls (you asked for it).

14 Sheets and pillowcases.

15 Shirts – white.

16 Shirts – striped.

17 Shirts – spotted.

18 Coloureds – fast.

19 Coloureds – slow.

20 Blacks.

21 Hats.

22 The dog.

23 Your teeth.

Your daughter's washing

24 Everything else.

25 All of Elsie McFarlane's washing because her machine has broken down and you don't fancy her things mixed up with yours.

Day 2. Not enough to wash

Day 5. Too much to wash

How to recognise piles of washing

So now you have the entire upstairs of the house strewn with piles of washing. If an average wash cycle in the machine takes 40 mins, how many hours continuous washing have you got? No, not $16^1/_2$ hours. The right answer is two weeks.

This is because of the Progressive Elongation of Loading/ Unloading Time Factor (PEOLUTF). It may only take five minutes to unload and reload between the first two loads, but between the last two loads it seems to take three days. This isn't really your fault. You shouldn't take on too much, you know. You also run out of washing powder (several times) and you have severe problems with drying and with clothes pegs. Just when you've got another load ready to hang out you find you've no more pegs left. You wish a gypsy woman would appear at the door with some pegs. There is a knock. It is some gypsies. They offer to macadam your drive quite cheaply or to take away your car for £5 (if you give them £5, of course). You dare not ask about clothes pegs in case they take offence at the technological insult.

You think through all this as you have a cup of coffee and read the newspaper. You realise you will have to run some loads together. Compromise, the story of your life. Then, if you think a bit harder, you realise that if you're smart you can run the wash in remarkably few loads. All women, including your wife, know this. They just start off telling you you've got to keep *those* separate! And *that* must always be done on half spin! Look how nice it's stayed because it's always been washed carefully. You don't tell her you put it through on full spin the last two weeks.

Anyway, here it is. The Basic Washing Pile System (BAWPS). This will save you hours of time and years of useful productive life (the same thing).

1 White things which are supposed to stay white.
2 Woolly things which are supposed to stay woolly.
3 Things which run. Usually tracksuits.*
4 Everything else.

* This is not a joke.

You may like to consider a few little test questions on the Basic Washing Pile System. This is to prepare you for those real-life problems waiting for you tomorrow, today. OK, fire away.

Q. Which pile do you put your wife's white silk blouse in?
A. Pile 1.
Q. Fool, nincompoop! You don't wash silk, you get it cleaned. £6 a time. Or you could try cleaning it yourself with a rag and some turps.

Q. Which pile do you put your underpants in?
A. Pile 2.
Q. Wrong! Pile 4.
A. They are woolly ones.
Q. They were once. Pile 4.

Q. Which pile do you put your tracksuit in?
A. Pile 3.
Q. Wrong! The dustbin.

Q. Which pile do you put your wife's pink nightie in?
A. Pile 4.
Q. Wrong! Pile 3, special setting for Delicates, use one spoonful Softikins washpowder plus rinse cycle additive Mogrose downy nap restorer squeeze gently by hand roll in a warm towel and spread over dog's back to dry.
A. Oh.

Well, you didn't do very well with those, did you? Never mind. If you are humble and humorous you may mess up the washing but your wife will still be tender with you after a large gin and tonic.

But have confidence. You can do it. In fact the only other things you need know about running the washing machine are these.

1 Just as you are about to go out, run lightly upstairs, seize one of your Basic Piles (which are, of course, sitting ready; the laundry basket stays empty most of the time) and stuff a load into the washing machine to run while you are out.

2 Ditto when you are going to bed or about to serve dinner. But beware of jiggles in the television picture caused by the machine trying to rinse your No. 4 pile.

Casual loading like this when you are really about to do something else creates a very good impression. It suggests you can handle the washing without appearing to think about it.

Then when you come in later or come down next morning you can take the washing out. Meanwhile you have forgotten where the machine is up to and when you open the door the water cascades out.

Effects of washing machine on television picture

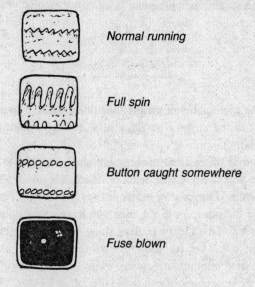

Normal running

Full spin

Button caught somewhere

Fuse blown

Getting things dry

After you have recovered from chuckling to yourself and humming while you mop the floor, you can take the washing out of the machine. Some bits are always tangled up and pull out other bits you don't want yet, which fall on the floor in front of the machine.

As this happens often the floor here is cleanish, but you can pick off the odd bit of fluff or matchstick.

Getting things dry, to a man, seems absurdly simple. You leave them around until they are. You don't share the woman's urge to own a tumble dryer. You don't even share her rage when it rains. You are a philosopher. If you hang the clothes out and it rains, why, you leave them longer. You ignore the bird droppings on the sheets.

The best way to dry things is to drape them all round the house on the radiators. This process humidifies the house and is good for your nasal passages.

When the clothes are dry, or nearly dry, you have to iron them. Ah! This is where our story really begins.

Iron in the soul

Iron the clothes by all means, but don't make a meal of it.

That is our motto – noble, a little defiant, committed, yet detached.

The first thing about ironing is that if the clothes are dry you have to wet them again. Sprinkle them. Or not if you have a steam iron. Things iron better if they are damp. The iron dries most of the damp out, but then you have to air them. You remember. This means putting them in the airing cupboard in neat flat piles. Or draping them around again.

The wise man makes ironing easier by adopting the following rules: what you might call iron rules. Indeed they cheer you up just to read them.

1 Only iron some of the things.
2 Only iron the fronts of things.
3 Don't iron things while you are wearing them.

Let us see how these rules work in practice.

1 *Only iron some of the things*. Well, you're not going to iron

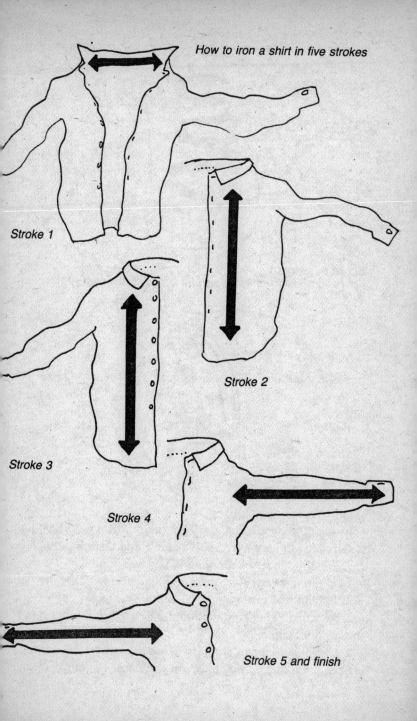

How to iron a shirt in five strokes

Stroke 1

Stroke 2

Stroke 3

Stroke 4

Stroke 5 and finish

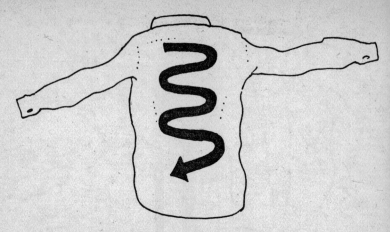

Stroke 6 (optional).
For perfection a sixth stroke can be added on the back

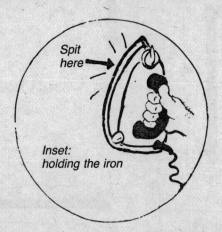

Spit
here

Inset:
holding the iron

your socks, are you? You are? Have it your own way. But
underpants, for example. You wouldn't iron them, would you?
. . . ? Well, don't. We're trying to save you trouble.

Don't iron sheets. Fold them and hang them so they dry flat.
You have to iron pillowcases . . . and napkins and
handkerchiefs. They're small and square and easy. You can go
to town on them.

2 *Only iron the fronts of things.* Shirts are what we're thinking
of. See the accompanying technical diagrams. Of course, if you

(a) How to iron a shirt in two strokes.

This method is favoured by barristers

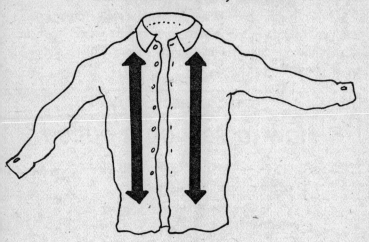

(b) How to iron a shirt in one stroke.

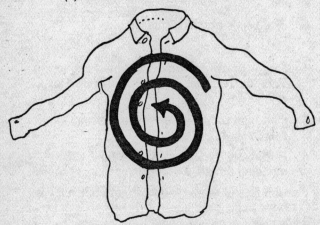

*Favoured by car salesmen but not recommended.
We consider it a rather splapdash short cut*

are going to sit in your office in your shirtsleeves, with
secretaries and female executives and bosses and even men
looking at your back, then you'd better iron the back of your

shirts. No point in being a laughing stock or letting them think your wife doesn't look after you properly.

3 *Don't iron things while you are wearing them.* In particular don't try to get a crease in your trousers without taking them off. On the other hand, don't do any ironing without your trousers on. Very risky.

TECHNICAL CHECKLIST NO. 2

How to sew on a button

in about twenty moderately easy stages

1 Locate garment requiring button.

2 Decide whether to detach garment from person inside it.

3 Glance expertly at other buttons, buttonholes, colour of thread, number of holes in buttons, etc.

4 Find wife's mending basket.

Or:

4a Find your own ex-Boy Scout mending kit. Very touching but put it back and look for wife's.

5 Find big trusty needle with a hole you can see through.

6 Find trusty thick black Neva-Brake cotton mending thread.

7 Wet end of thread in mouth and pinch it flat between fingers.

8 Thread needle quickly and deftly.

9 Double up thread and tie ends together with a few knots so thread doesn't come through material.

10 Go looking for a button. Look on ledges, mantelpiece, etc. Where *recent* buttons are put. Look in your nut-and-bolt jar.

11 Find button.

12 Stitch secure anchorage point on garment.

13 Drop button down thread. This is a nice moment in the process. Make the most of it.

14 Put generous number of stitches through holes in button. When trying to poke needle up through holes, be ready to prick fingers. Note that you only bleed on white garments.

15 Bring thread out at side between button and material. Wind thread round and round to make a sort of stalk, until button looks like African native with elongated neck.

16 Take thread back underneath and secure with various loops and knots.

17 Cut thread.

18 Try to do up button. Find it won't go through buttonhole.

19 Experience unexpected flow of adrenalin through system. Hear own teeth grinding.

Either:

20 Cut button off and go back to 3. Glance expertly, etc.

Or:

20a Deftly enlarge buttonhole with scissors.

Mending

Now you have got things ironed and you are lovingly sorting clothes into yet more piles and putting them into drawers for your dear family.

You may discover the following minor faults awaiting repair.

We offer these examples – not all may occur together – to provide a full and testing range to challenge your skills.

1 A button off your shirt.
2 A button off your daughter's school blouse.
3 In fact several buttons off several things.
4 A hole in the knee of your son's trousers.
5 The zip coming out of your trousers.
6 Somebody has put a foot through the sheet on your bed!
7 The lace at the neck of your wife's aubergine-coloured Tom Jones-style ruffled shirt has been snagged by something (probably your neighbour's finger nail).

To help you deal with these trivial problems you have the following technologies at your disposal:

(a) Needle and thread.
(b) Glue.
(c) Stapling.

So far so good. But which do you use for which?

Buttons. See nearby checklist for sewing buttons on neatly and slowly, or quickly and grotesquely. Buttons, like most of us, are subject to certain laws, e.g.

★ You can only sew on one button a week. (Usually at 8.35 on Monday morning.)
★ You can always find lots of spare buttons which are slightly too big for the buttonhole.

These laws mean that if you have children you can never sew your own buttons on. Keep a supply of small safety pins.

Fun with glue. Glue is a greatly undervalued mending material. Buy a certain rubbery kind of glue which is supposedly good for mending carpets. And there you are. A hole in some trousers? Cut a patch of like material – from an unregarded part of the trousers if you can find one – and glue the patch on. Glue it on the inside, not the outside; unless you can't find any similar material, in which case take something nice and bright, glue it on the outside and make a feature of it. Your son will be so admired by his schoolmates. A hole in the sheet? Easy. Glue a patch over it. Find a really interesting piece of material to liven up the old sheet, like a square of corduroy. Make a professional job of it by running adhesive tape round the edge.

Stapling. Zip coming out of your trousers? Easy. Staple it back in place. Don't go to the lavatory.

Tatting. Repairing your wife's lacy somethings? Could be tricky. You may have to revive your old tatting skills.* It is the quiet time of the evening. The children are in bed or doing their jigsaws. Your wife is at a marketing conference. In the mellow light of the table lamp you are sitting tatting. Your strong clever fingers form the string irrevocably into delicate shapes. Then you take up your wife's thingy and fit the new piece of tracery into the torn lace edging. Humming an old folk tune your mother taught you, you secure the new piece with tiny invisible stitches. You put the garment carefully on the floor and stamp on it a few times. This ancient trick makes the new lace look just like the old.

Suddenly the back door slams. Your wife appears in the doorway. She hurls her briefcase into a corner and leans against the sideboard. No! And yet – could that be the smell of whisky on her breath? Again?

* Tatting: a sort of embroidery with string. Nothing to do with the expression 'old tat'.

5
Cooking
or
Say it with potatoes

IT'S STRANGE but true that men can enjoy cooking more than
women. They don't feel it as so much of an unremitting
burden. They distinguish more clearly than women the two
sides of cooking in the home: what is duty and what is not.
They don't take duty as seriously and draw more pleasure from
what is not duty.

Naturally there are things you have to learn. To be precise,
it is more a matter of accustoming yourself. You have to get
used to being around in the kitchen. You have to get used to
knocking up something to eat without making a meal of it.*

You should enjoy two things. Enjoy simply being in your
kitchen. And enjoy eating what you cook. That way you are
not torn apart; you add quality to what you do.

You may have to sort your kitchen out a bit first. Perhaps
you are in charge of the house, but only intermittently. Here
too there is a transition stage. You have to get back into it.
You should know where things are and what you've got and
what you like. In the kitchen there is a great opportunity for a
man's natural style to find expression. You should let this
happen, you'll find it very satisfying. Your family may start off
being amused by your habits or idiosyncrasies or preferences.
In the end they'll value the best of them more than you realise.
You'll soon find out what they don't like.

And remember, if you haven't worked it out already, that
the art of cooking is the art of disguise – at least as far as

---

* This may be a joke.

you're concerned. We're not talking about coarse cooking. That's just a rugby club joke. You can do better than the baked bean syndrome. At the other extreme we're not concerned with professional-type chefing. You're not the sort of chap who points out that nearly all the great chefs are men and who won't let your wife come in the kitchen because she cuts cake with your Sabatier knife.

But you have to take stock of your limitations. Perhaps you can only make four basic things. Perhaps you are, dare we say it, inclined to be lazy or at any rate very relaxed. This is where the art of disguise comes in. You learn to ring the variations on your four basic dishes. You learn to decorate them and flavour them. And remember the other art, even if right now you aren't preparing a little something for your mistress: the art of cooking is also the art of seduction. More of that later.

Back to basics, again

The point isn't really whether you can or can't cook, as if cooking were like swimming. The point is that you have to feed the family. Even more to the point, you have to nourish them. This is what you should consider for five minutes. Ask the following questions:

- What do you like?
- What agrees with you?
- What gives balance?
- What is economical?

Your personal economics dictate in part what you can and can't buy, but by no means all. Hands up those who think fish and chips is still a cheap meal. So forget about false economies. You will find that basic questions generate simple answers and that you can eat quite cheaply and well at home.

You will even find, by the end of this chapter, that

surprisingly little 'cooking' need be involved. Preparation, yes. You need to give time and attention to preparing food. You will get a lot of pleasure from it.

You can throw the Sunday roast out of the window – almost: leave it on the windowsill for the time being (or where the cat can't get it). So many of us grew up with fixed and elaborate routines. Old-style Sunday lunch has many virtues. It unites the family. It builds you up. But it makes a slave out of the wife. Men who insist on their Sunday roasts should cook it all themselves from time to time. It's not as if it's difficult: it cooks itself while you're at church . . .

Start listening to your own body system more carefully. Eat less rather than more. Stay a little hungry and feel keener and more energetic. Discover that small amounts of really tasty food are more satisfying than the opposite.

So out you go to buy food. Buy the basics. Buy good bread (or make it!). Buy lots of fruit and vegetables. Such a pleasure, shopping in a greengrocer's. For your money you get a lot of stuff – a big boxful. The curious thing is that you'll find (by the end of the chapter . . .) that you're buying less meat. But don't forget to ask the butcher for some bones for the dog. Make soup with them first.

You'll find out, you'll be forcibly reminded, that children are always hungry. They say they are when they can't be, and then they are. So give 'em plenty, poor little mites. Their mum out at work, 'n all.

Friends in the kitchen

Your best friend among foods is undoubtedly the onion.

For a start the onion is beautiful, whichever way you peel or slice it. Who cares about stinging eyes? The onion is a pleasure to handle and prepare. Allow your hands to enjoy it. Be satisfied by its roundness. Later you can sniff your fingers and find an agreeable onion smell on them.

Then you can do so many things with your onion. Boil it,
roast it, fry it, chop it up and eat it raw. Add it to practically
everything. One of our favourite neighbours is eighty-four and
she walks round the block and eats a raw onion every day. We
kiss her and she never smells of onion, not that we would care.
But your smell depends more on your soul than on the onion.
Think hard before you ripost. If you are in a harmonious state,
you digest better.

Herbs are special friends too. Herbs cover a multitude of
sins. Remember that a man succeeds in the kitchen largely
with the aid of cunning. Indeed, this applies to the whole
problem of being left alone to run the house. It's no good
being painstaking and honest. You will only wear yourself out
and not be much further forward. You've got to be sprightly
and good company for everybody – including yourself, so
resort to low cunning. This is where herbs come in.

You need a pot of mixed herbs at least, plus some others –
basil is our favourite. Try inviting the neighbours for lunch,
cook some sausages, plaster them with herbs, serve with brown
bread and mustard and declare that they are tasting the famous
Scented Sausage from Silesia; or the no-less-famous Wafting
Wurst from Württemburg. Well, try it anyway.

Then there is garlic. You add garlic to everything you
haven't already added onions to. You can also add garlic to
onions or onions to garlic. Peeling and chopping garlic is an
even greater pleasure, if this is possible, than peeling onions.
You can die of pleasure from garlic. You thought this only
happened to French prime ministers in brothels. Garlic is the
strongest card in the low cunning pack. A garlicky cooking
smell immediately creates a wondrous French-family-kitchen-
type atmosphere and causes neighbours to say to your wife,
'Aren't you lucky?'

Trying to convey more than words alone impart, she
answers, 'Yes. But it does get upstairs.'

The neighbour mis-hears this and doesn't realise your wife is
talking about the smell. Next morning you have someone

← *A clove of garlic. Remember to crunch a bit up in the morning to get rid of that stale, overnight taste*

Give zest to those everyday dishes by adding garlic to:

Cheese on toast

Pilchards

Stewed apple

Baked beans

Things you can add garlic to

coming for coffee so you start preparing lunch early to get the smell going again. From time to time you bump into the string of garlic you have picturesquely hung from the kitchen ceiling.

Days, weeks pass. You devote yourself to your cooking. Calmly, purposefully, you move about the kitchen selecting, peeling, chopping, mixing, pouring, stirring, tasting. Your only problem is how to get it all into the frying pan.*

Just as a racing driver is at one with the controls of his

* Buy another.

machine, just as horse and rider share a common understanding, so you and your frying pan are perfectly attuned. In the kitchen, the frying pan is man's best friend (with respect to onions and dogs). You can do practically anything with a frying pan. True art with the frying pan means cooking things in it so they don't look fried. The man in the kitchen has a basic hurdle to get over: his wife thinks his efforts taste quite nice, but they lack a bit of variety. So you've got to get variety out of your frying pan. You can always try adding some colouring. A green fried egg wakes people up in the mornings even if they don't eat the egg. The dog will always eat it as he's colour blind.

Perhaps by now you have got a wok. No? It's time you wok up.* Woks are good for men to cook with because they operate on the frying pan principle but are more refined. Wives approve of them because they cook vegetables well. They do. You do something in a wok called stir-frying. When you have done this you do some fry-stirring. Then you put it on a plate and start fry-eating.

Things you can do with . . .

The following suggestions are the merest selection of possibilities open to you. We're not writing a cookbook, we just wanted to give you the general idea. To encourage and inspire.

Carrots. Peel, cut lengthwise into strips, put in front of children while they watch television. Shows commendable awareness that carrots are good for teeth, hair, eyes, toenails, earlobes, etc.

* This sentence should read: It's time you oke up.

Item	Before
Rice pudding	
Roast chicken	
Boar's head	
Spare ribs	

After	**Comments**

Make into a delightful individual trifle. Add glace cherry and a sprig of mint

Forget and leave in oven for a week. Make a warm nourishing tasty broth with a stock cube

Sprinkle fresh parsley on top and try again. Remove bent fork

Give the dog a treat. Shut him outside afterwards

Leftovers and what to do with them

Celery. Celery is a virtuous vegetable, stuck there in its jug on the table. Take it out of the jug, cut it up, boil it lightly and serve with butter. The kids won't like it (they didn't anyway) but you will.

Eggs. Keep a supply of hardboiled eggs in the fridge. Then you can mix them with other things like mayonnaise or rice (see below).

Fish. Buy some real fish one day. It doesn't matter what kind. It's usually white and flat. And cheaper than meat. Put it in the frying pan (what else?), cover it with milk, add butter, chopped garlic and simmer. Divine.

Fruit. The kids always eat it, healthy little devils. Give in and buy some more. Experience teaches you to hide some apples (and chocolate) in case you want some yourself.

Leeks. Big leeks are handy for tickling your wife with. Leeks have a wonderful taste too. Boil them up, eat them in a sauce (see below) or straight with butter and black pepper or cold in a vinaigrette.

Leftovers. There is a whole book in leftovers. The artful housewife (i.e. you) always has leftovers. If you look in the fridge or in the cupboard there should be some leftovers for you to turn into something delicious. For example, there may be some chicken bits left. Or there may be some cold potato which you can fry up. Or there may be some cold rice pudding, etc.

NB. To have leftovers you have to cook quite a lot in the first instance and then not eat it all. This doesn't seem to happen much in our house as the hyenas, sorry, children eat everything. It's not worth making pseudo-leftovers specially but see also Rice.

Mayonnaise. Very good for exquisite grown-up-type snacks. You have to buy the expensive continental sort. You put some dollops of it in a bowl. Beat a little cooking oil into it, this lightens and dilutes it. You can add top of the milk likewise. Then you squeeze garlic into it (through the garlic press): wonderful with avocado pears, salads, cold meats, baked potatoes.

Next day you do the same and add a small amount of curry paste: superb with hardboiled eggs; quite good just eaten with brown bread and butter.

Or you can add chopped onion. I haven't mentioned onion for some time.

Meat. Well, it's nice to have some meat for a change. When you're passing the butcher, go in and buy some meat. It doesn't matter what.

All right: you think you will appear absurd and amateurish if you queue up in the butcher's with all the other housewives and say, 'Please could I have some meat?' Suddenly there will be silence in the shop. Then a chuckle from the back of the queue. The butcher's face for a moment will be a polite blank of disbelief. Then he throws back his head amid roars of laughter. The queue collapses amid shrieks of mirth. Strangers cling together and wipe their eyes.

To avoid this happening you should ask for a pound and a half of pork fillet. If he says he hasn't any, you say, 'Some lamb, then?'

Whatever it is, when you get it home you cut it into small lumps or strips. Cook it in oil in your wok. Add salt and pepper. Add chopped veg, e.g. onion, green pepper, aubergine, mushroom, garlic. Add some milk. Add some wine. Put the lid on and let it simmer for a while. Prepare for ecstasy. Eat it.

Mushrooms. Mushrooms are another real pal in the kitchen. You can fry them up in no time, you can add them to things, you can chop them raw in salads. What a funny word mushroom is if you look at it.

Potatoes. Buy pre-washed ones. Then you don't need to peel them, just cut nasty bits out. Tell the family all the vitamins are in the skin.

Cut them ultra thin. You can do this by hand on your chopping board or in your wife's curiously named food processor, assuming you are allowed to use it. But you are supposed to be in charge round here. Anyway slice the potatoes thinly, then you can fry them rapidly and deliciously. If you are after sophistication you bake them in the oven, having covered them with milk, garlic, cheese or whatever.

Rice. Very good to have around. Buy whole-grain rice; it looks nicer, tastes nicer and does no end of good to your bowel. Enliven the rice with your usual panoply of bits of veg, ham, olives. It's easy to do too much rice so you stand a good chance of having leftovers.

Sauce. You know how to make a sauce. Melt butter in a pan, mix some flour with it, pinch of salt, add water and/or milk, keep stirring so there are no lumps. Then you can add other things like grated cheese or . . . tuna fish.

Tuna fish. Tuna fish in tins is one of the great inventions of our age. For many people tuna fish brings back memories of picnics in scenic laybys on holidays in France. For the opportunist man about the house, tuna fish signals the answers to a hundred problems of what to give 'em. The secret of tuna fish is that it goes with everything. Salads, potatoes, rice, sauces, ice cream, eggs, vegetables, sandwiches, the list is all but endless, or at any rate quite long.

Vegetables. The thing with vegetables is not to overcook them. Boil them for the least amount of time in the least amount of water. Cabbage, sprouts, cauli – those old stagers become young lyrical fruits of the earth. Fresh, tasty and chewy. Remember that pans boil dry quicker if you don't put much water in.

Knocking something up

This is the first kind of cooking. It means getting something palatable dished up quickly. You particularly have to do it for children. If you do it all the time your life is lacking in romance.

If you have to feed the five thousand and come up smiling you need stand-bys. There are good old stand-bys like shepherd's pie: mince covered with mashed potato; stew; soups. Make your own soups in the pressure cooker. There are simple classic dishes like: buy some ham; boil potatoes and serve with butter; add frozen peas.

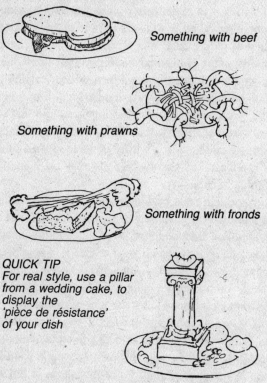

Something with beef

Something with prawns

Something with fronds

QUICK TIP
For real style, use a pillar
from a wedding cake, to
display the
'pièce de résistance'
of your dish

Some tasty main course suggestions

Our children like certain things out of tins. We tend to spurn baked beans although they are liked. They have their place, be not proud. One child has a tomato sauce fetish. But what drives them crazy is meat balls. If you announce meat balls they begin to bounce up and down and ricochet around the room. We are grateful to meat balls for giving so much pleasure. For some reason meat balls seem to come from Bulgaria. Perhaps Bulgars are good at basketball.

Sometimes we serve ravioli. Sweetcorn and our old friend tuna fish, especially mixed, can have an electrifying but finally soporific effect.

It's a good idea to have one or two specialities. The family will love you for them if they're edible.

In our family – to my surprise – the children become excited when something called powerfood is announced. It contains things they wouldn't eat if they were served in other forms. Powerfood is a sort of mishmash. Naturally it is fried, though it can be wokked. It usually has a potato base, though it can have a rice base. It nearly always has garlic in it and nearly always has onions in it. Then it has anything else that's going, vegetables such as peppers, leeks or mushrooms, or meat or chicken bits. Sometimes it's a fishy powerfood with tuna fish or prawns for a treat. It's slightly oily and very tasty and filling and extremely satisfactory.

Another speciality is a pudding called a daddy pudding. It's not so much a pudding, more a process. You start with dollops of ice cream. You then add a series of other ingredients. All are optional and variable. Like all good dishes it is best prepared under the eyes of the hopeful recipients. On top of the ice cream you add a prehensile blob of golden syrup. You can try treacle but not every one likes it; or jam or marmalade. Then a handful of sultanas. It helps the effect if you hurl them at the pudding. Then you pour milk all over the repulsive but fascinating pile. Sprinkle some brown sugar on if you like the crunching. For kids add hundreds of thousands or Smarties. For persons of responsible age pour rum over the top.

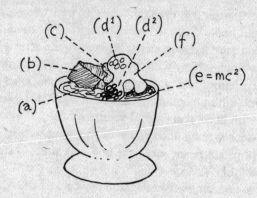

Devilling something up

Devilling something up is totally different from knocking something up. You devil something up for the hell of it. This is when you are really cooking for yourself or for your pal. This is the other kind of cooking, the kind you enjoy, this kind entails standing round drinking and smoking and stirring things.

If you don't smoke, at least you won't drop ash in the powerfood. If you don't drink you may have problems as you have to pour wine into some dishes.

This is where you knock up – sorry, devil up, your tricky mayonnaise mixtures. You have been at home all morning, working hard. You've taken the rubbish out. You've practised your flower arrangement for the WI. Now you have a visitor coming for lunch. How indiscreet! How discreet! What will you serve? Avocadoes with prawn filling and salad? Or perhaps the simple but devastating caviar (well, lump fish roe) with fingers of toast and tumblers of neat vodka? Follow that up with some cold meats from the deli, plus one of your disguised leftover specials, a potato and onion mix, washed down with a very young Beaujolais, and the two of you will have absolutely had your chips.

Or once again it is evening. The children are tucked up in bed. You, dressed in your tasselled caftan, are meditating near the frying pan. You are awaiting your wife. She is a little late, she is in town talking with finance people. What will you serve? Perhaps a bed of brown rice, simmering even now with herbs and a hint of nutmeg. And on it some diced spicy lamb served with cucumber in cold yogurt.

The door is flung open and suddenly your wife is in the room. Impatiently she kicks the dog as it affectionately sniffs her boots. She speaks.

'Those goddamn accountants! They cocked the whole f****** deal up with their footling smart-arse tactics, unbelievable bloody ignorant lot and here am I working my tits off—'

'Darling,' you interject mildly, 'how disappointing. But never mind. Perhaps you can set it up again—'

'Oh, shut up! What do you know about it?'

'There, dearest, now you're home again and you can relax. I've got some tasty diced spicy lamb on brown rice ready for you.' You smile and look in the wok or wherever the diced spicy, etc. is.

'Diced spicy lamb on brown rice?' your wife shouts. 'You can stuff that! I'm going to bed. I ate in town anyway.'

With that she vanishes upstairs. You eat some of the diced spicy, etc. and wedge the rest in with the other leftovers in the fridge.

Yes, you reflect, cooking can be a wonderful sexual stimulant between men and women. But the attraction doesn't always depend on avocadoes or prawns or vodka. Quite a lot can result from marmalade sandwiches in the night. The main thing is, you say to yourself as you drink another tumblerful of cooking vodka, the main thing is, the timing has to be right.

6
Pet management

or
Who leads the dog's life?

NOW THAT YOU are at home more than anyone else, you have the job of looking after the family's pets. If you haven't any pets in your family, you can sigh and say that of course you're an animal lover really.

If you have got pets, you can sigh and say that you always thought you were an animal lover – until this.

It isn't made any easier by your children. My daughter likes to rehearse a list of the people she loves best in the world. I am putting her to bed. I gaze into her bright face and wistful eyes as she considers the ranks of her loved ones. The list usually goes something like this:

No. 1 and most of all in the world: Mummy.
    2 The dog.
    3 Her brother.
    4 The cat.
    5 Various grannies, grandpas, etc. all breasting the tape
      together.
    6 The goldfish.

I wait politely. 'Yes, darling?' I say. Perhaps I am No. 7. That would be better than nothing.

'Oh, Dad!' she says. 'I forgot about you. Would you mind very much if I love you the same as George?' George is the dog. Well, second equal is quite good really. It's just that . . . if you knew what I really thought of the dog you'd understand.

I do *try* to love the dog. A little halfheartedly, I admit. If he were someone else's dog I might think he was wonderful, great fun, adorable, so naughty, so appealing. The problem is that I feel responsible for the brute. But he conflicts with my idea of what is proper and orderly behaviour. I try to remind myself to stay detached and not care. It's quite hard to when you come down in the morning and find he has crapped on the carpet. Again. Yes, I know. It's good for you to be humble and learn philosophy from a dog.

Did you say we've got his routine wrong? But he always wants to go out at 2.30 a.m.

Types of mess and what to do about them

Animals have a lot of ways of messing things up. It's best if you discover messes after you have had a drink in the evening and you don't care particularly. But usually you have to deal with mess in the mornings when you don't feel quite comfortable in your skin and neurotically require things to be clean and tidy. You reflect savagely that animals and children are programmed to turn order into disorder. You ask yourself what would happen if you didn't clean and pick things up. You have a vision of all the objects in the house becoming rearranged in a random litter several feet deep and covered in filth; with you trapped underneath it somewhere. All this in accordance with the second law of thermodynamics as the universe slowly degenerates into an undifferentiated soup of stagnant matter. You think it's speeding up a bit in your house.

Common categories of mess are the following. Note how Sod's Law always tends to operate, viz. messes arise where places are cleanest or after you have just cleaned and not before you were going to.

1 *Muddy paw marks*. Relatively harmless. You can manage a tired, frigid smile over this kind of mess. It does get a bit

Loveable things pets do

boring when you find the cat's paw marks all over the kitchen table and the working surfaces and the fridge top and the windowsills *every* morning. You wonder what occult exercise the cat gets up to at night which makes it walk about on everything so thoroughly. Wipe the paw marks. Then rinse the dish cloth. Pretend it's not the dish cloth if anyone notices.

2 *Mouse innards*. Our cat seems to eat the entire mouse with the exception of a particular bit of gut. Perhaps it's the gall bladder, or the large intestine. It's not very big but always the same bit. On mornings when you come downstairs without your slippers on you tread on it. If it's not in the way, the thing to do is leave it for a day. Then it goes hard and dry and it's not as yukky to pick up.

3 *Animal hair or fur*. Quite simple really: you vacuum the carpet. Then you vacuum round the skirting board and in the corners. Then you vacuum under the furniture. Then you vacuum the furniture. You take the cushions out and vacuum down the cracks. You take the cushion covers off because of bits of hairy gunge on them. If you're lucky you wash them. Otherwise they go to the cleaners. Then you look at some of your clothes. You shake them outside. You try to vacuum them, but they get stuck up the nozzle. You try to vacuum the dog, but he bites the vacuum and runs away.

4 *Jobs*. What? Oh. Just pray that your dog's bowels stay in good order. Then you can go on using the dust pan and brush. Pray you will be spared starting the day on your knees in the middle of the sitting-room carpet with the kitchen roll, the carpet shampoo and the disinfectant.

5 *Piddle*. Only somewhat annoying, unless it's tom cat piddle, which stinks. If it's your cat, have him castrated quick. If it's other cats coming after your cat, have her spayed and keep them out.

6 *Puke*. The less said about this the better. Just hope it's only grass and saliva and nothing nasty. Also hope the beast wasn't trotting along while it puked.

There are certain other manifestations of your pets' presence which come into the nuisance category. One of these is smell.

As dogs do, our dog farts from time to time. This would not be remarkable except that he looks round in surprise to see where the noise came from.

Some dogs like rolling in carrion. If they find a dead rabbit, as well as eating it they will roll on it. Or in manure. Then your pet trots into the house and wags his tail and jumps up and is affectionate towards everybody. You come in and find the children stroking him. This is when you remind your wife that the dog should live in the shed and be a proper dog, not a lap dog. Your wife gets cross and says he's only a dog and you don't love him. It occurs to you to invite her to choose between him and you, but you decide not to press the matter.

Pet cursing

You are in charge of running the house. Or at least you've just cleaned the place up a bit. Then the animals rush in and mess things up deliberately. This is where pet cursing comes in.

It's the same old story. You're responsible for something but not in control of it. What do you do? You learn controlled cursing and kicking – same as with your children, basically. Pet cursing can be quite enjoyable, even though you are in a rage at the time, and it does help to prevent you becoming bitter and negative.

A story is told of a man who lived in the East and whose job it was to get up very early every day and sound a steam whistle in order to wake the citizens up and get them off to work. He began to feel unwell; he wasn't actually ill, he just felt very low indeed. This state of affairs persisted for a couple of years. Finally it came to him why he felt so bad: when he sounded his steam whistle to wake up the town, the oaths and revilements of the entire population were directed at the individual who disturbed their peace. So he began, before he released his steam whistle, to release a volley of foul and violent curses upon the citizens of the town, in order to rebut the psychic torrent of malice which was again about to be launched upon him. He did this every day and ever after felt much better.

This story gives you the clue about pet cursing; indeed, about rebutting negativity and hostility more widely. After your animal has done something unspeakable and you have to clear it up, curse the animal and its effects and its progeny and its forebears long, loudly and explicitly. Remember to do it as consciously as you can, then it will do you some good. You will be in a rage, but don't be in a blind rage. Say to yourself, 'I am in a rage and I am cursing this animal and in a few moments I will feel better.' Curse particularly foully while you are doing the mopping up.

This way you get tensions out of your system and later you will be able to laugh about it. Well, eventually. The other approach is to expect your little four-legged darlings to have fouled the place up and then when they haven't, you're pleased. This is foolish and the wrong way round.

Pet kicking

Pet kicking is a rather refined skill, which allows you to express certain emotions and which also confirms the animal's own perception of the family pecking order.

The technique is mostly applied to dogs who, when being chastised, tuck their tails in and assume a roundness at the rear end. Since some dogs are, while entirely loveable, also irrepressible, when you are opening the door a crack to the paper boy or the postman or the milkman, the dog roars past you and merrily leaps upon the hapless deliverer in order to test his cuffs and pocket flaps with sharp nips. This is an occasion for the kick.

'Go to your bed, sir!' you order. Reluctantly the dog relinquishes his friend (he does it every day) and scuttles past you, guarding his rear end. Quick as a flash you swivel and with the instep of your slippered foot you punt the luckless beast on its way to its basket. The dog, propelled magically onward in this manner, reflects on its good fortune in having its master pay any attention to it at all, and comes back to pay court to you, wagging its tail, wrinkling its muzzle and baring its teeth in a subservient grin.

If you and the dog practise you can perfect the slippered punt so that you put a spin on it and it works round corners, rather in the style of a Bobby Charlton striking a curling banana shot from outside the penalty area.

But there are intractable disciplinary problems. Cake stealing

Kicking the dog

(a) Straight – the slippered punt

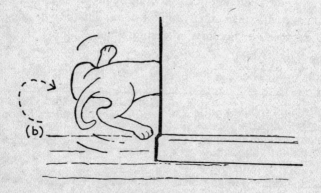

(b) Round corners.
Illustrated: the outswinger

is one. You leave a cake or some cheese on the table. Next thing you know – nothing. Gone. No evidence. The dog wags his tail at you. What do you do? Beat the dog? Show him a picture of a cake? Not feed him for two days? Whatever you do, he wags his tail. Best thing is to make another cake.

Duties to pets

If you own a pet you have various obligations to it, if you are conscientious. The obligations mostly fall on the housewife (you).

Walking the dog is one of the classic duties. There are various ways of not walking the dog. We assume that you haven't time – you are just too overburdened with housework. In between pursuing your part-time career and getting some sleep, taking the dog out, reluctantly, regretfully, just can't be a priority. The thing to have is a self-propelling dog. This is a dog which runs round of its own accord. Whether you can let it depends on where you live. Perhaps you can train it to go to the newsagent or the library or trot off for a check-up at the vet's. The other thing, the only other thing, you can do is bribe people to take the dog out. You start with your own children, then certain categories of other people's children, then your wife, then other people's wives. That is when dog walking suddenly becomes interesting again.

Cats

	First dose	Second dose after 7 days	Third dose after 21 days
Small cats up to 7 lb	2½ white tablets 1 yellow tablet	4 white tablets 3 yellow tablets	1 green tablet
Average cats 7–12 lb	3 white tablets 2½ yellow tablets	5½ white tablets 4¼ yellow tablets	2 green tablets
Large cats over 12 lb	4 white tablets 3½ yellow tablets	11 white tablets 5 yellow tablets	3 green tablets
Abnormally large cats and lions	27 white tablets 4½ yellow tablets	40 white tablets 20 yellow tablets	200 green tablets

Meanwhile you have to worm your pets. You have just wormed your kids, so you may as well worm the dog and cat too. You take down all the old packets of worm tablets. They all have one or two tablets left in them but you haven't enough yellow tablets so you have to buy another packet.

When you have remembered to do this a few weeks later you start again and you need the instructions. See the tables.

It is *very important* not to miss a dose. If you do, start again. (This instruction is really designed so that you go on dosing the wretched animal for ever and spend all the child allowance on worm tablets.)

After you have administered a random number of tablets to your pet, you realise you don't know how much it weighs. You put it on the bathroom scales but it jumps off. You put it on and hold it firmly. It weighs four stone. You must have been pressing slightly. Finally you remember. You undress, pick up the pet and stand on the scales. Nursing a nasty scratch, you work out the weight of your pet.

You then find it has puked up the tablet you thought it had swallowed. The vet can do it. He holds the cat's jaws so it looks like a viper, flicks a tablet in, strokes its throat, and down it goes. You pay on the way out.

Your cat won't do it at all. It either struggles furiously or goes all rigid, presumably thinking at last you have had enough of it. You speak reassuringly. The cat bites you. You grind up the tablets and look for something irresistible to mix them

Dogs

	First dose	*Second dose*	*Third dose*
Small dogs up to 4 oz	0.2 white tablet 0.55 yellow tablet	½ green tablet	10 big red tablets
Other dogs	1 or 2 white tablets A few yellow tablets	A handful of whatever's left	Don't bother

with. Not jam, this is the cat. Cat food? Not a hope, he smells the powder. Sardines? The cat tries them, then stares at you balefully and slinks off.

Hours can pass while you are thus involved in an intimate caring relationship with your animals.

Caring for your daughter's pony

We've no sympathy with you. Off you go again, out in the rain, with your bucket and fork and old blanket. Remember you're on the last bale. Yes, she did so want it . . . You forgot to ask yourself something. Did she even look after her goldfish?

Caring for your daughter's goldfish

No, she didn't. At least you can do this indoors. After a while you harden your heart and leave the lid off. You come down next morning. Empty! Where—? Your daughter cries. The cat blinks.

Problems with gerbils

At the end of term your offspring will probably volunteer to have the class gerbil home during the holidays. The only way to avoid this is to have had the gerbil for the previous holidays, during which it mysteriously and lamentably died. Then you never get asked again.

Conducting pets' funerals

If, heaven forbid, one of your pets should pass away, you have to be prepared to help the children assimilate the poor (or fortunate) creature's change of state. Children are often more matter-of-fact than adults about death and if the pet is put to sleep by the vet, you should bring it home for a burial ceremony. Then there is a satisfactory continuity and completion in the relationship between family and pet.

We used to have a faithful cat whose time came at the relatively early age of eleven. We brought him back from the vet packed neatly in a shoe box, a good class of British-made all-leather, hand-tooled shoe. My wife was away overnight (some business trip or other). The cat was left lying in state or more precisely in the shed in his shoe box. We wanted Mummy to see Blackie before he was buried. When Mummy got home next day Blackie was taken out of the shoe box to show her. He was rectangular.

The sarcophagus was dragged down the garden on a small trolley, accompanied by a melancholy procession. Bringing up the rear, one mourner keened the Funeral March, ignoring his wife's instructions to shut up. Then the shoe box was laid to rest and the grave filled in. A small cross was erected, although the cat was agnostic, saying: 'Blackie: a fine cat.' The children sprinkled flowers on the grave, wept and departed satisfied.

Pets are good for you

Perhaps the real question is whether you are good for your pet. But you try. You do your best. You buy the pet food. Sometimes you're relaxed and affectionate, and then how they dance around you! They think you're going to feed them.

If you're smart you buy the pet food in bulk at the supermarket. The girl at the check-out glances at the piles of tins in the trolley and asks if you have a lot of pets. You say no, the children like it.

Recent research has shown that pet owners live longer – presumably than non-pet owners. Nobody, of course, lives as long as shepherds in the Caucasus, where every one expires at the age of 131. It used to be thought they lived a long time because of the pure mountain air. Or because they were so happy being Soviet citizens. Perhaps it's really because they have sheep.

Effects of stroking your pet for health

(a)

(b)

(c)

Why do pet owners live longer? Because stroking pets lowers the blood pressure. And why is this? You might think that the sort of people who have pets are relaxed, loving people at peace with nature. No. It's the stroking, the exercise. Perhaps it expands the lungs.

This raises a lot of questions. It sounds as if the bigger the pet you have, the more stroking it can take without collapsing under a welter of caresses from keep-fit maniacs.

Anyway, off you go and stroke something. If you haven't got a pet, perhaps you could stroke your neighbour's pet or, failing that, your neighbour.

7
Neighbours
or
Charity begins next door

BE GRATEFUL to your neighbours. They often hold a mirror up to you. When you are good friends with them, that's fine. When you are not, remember the old saying: your adversary is your best friend. You can learn something about human nature, and about yourself, even from your neighbours.

If you're the old-fashioned kind of husband, who goes off to work and leaves the wife at home, you don't necessarily see much of the neighbours. You see them over the garden fence on evenings or at weekends and you see them socially for drinks or occasionally for dinner. A curious category of *bonhomie* often prevails with neighbours; especially emanating from the men. But a slight distance persists which preserves the neighbourly relationship.

But now you're involved with housewifely and maternal tasks. Perhaps you are at home more of the time. You meet, you have dealings with other mothers. The fact that you're a man naturally makes a difference. It creates a sort of problem. There is a sexual barrier, you don't have the same interests or exchange confidences and chit-chat in the same way as women do. You also begin to see what goes on between women.

You begin to detect the social nuances, the status indicators, the competition, the intimacies, jealousies and betrayals. Very quickly you discover the norms of behaviour and the cliques. You realise women inhabit their own various social jungles, as men do theirs.

This chapter will be your social guide. So you don't stay

shyly at home; so you don't tremble and blush as you collect the children; so you don't sit awkwardly in the corner at the nearly new coffee morning and realise you were invited by mistake because they thought you were your wife.

No, after reading this chapter you will be happy, confident and clear-sighted. Actually as the man among women you have a great advantage. You are untouched by many of their particular tribulations. Your psychology is different.

What they worry about you don't. What they grumble about you don't. You know something they don't. You may have got up and made breakfast and dressed the children and transported them and been shopping and done some cleaning and got lunch ready and so on. But you don't take it seriously. Nor do you take them or yourself too seriously. Through the veils of hassle, anxiety and gossip you calmly proceed, unmoved . . . thinking your wife gets home the day after tomorrow and takes over again, thank heavens.

The school run

The school run brings you into contact with many puzzling questions.

Why, for example, does nobody speak to you while you stand waiting at the school gate? Is it because you are a man? Perhaps your breath smells? Or your flies are undone? No, it's not those. You thought that because you were a man the other mothers would flock round you like moths round a light, chatting amiably and amusingly. Didn't you? Well, you hoped it. And? They ignore you totally. As a mother approaches you prepare a gaze and a faint smile of readiness, but she floats through it with eyes fixed towards a more distant object.

What is wrong with you? you wonder. Can it be the car? You did notice some children laughing at it the other day because it is so quaint and rusty. Perhaps it *is* you. Perhaps

Children laugh at your car. Or at you?

you're different. You make them uneasy. You'd better take the initiative. Smile, chat, make some friends. It does make a little difference. You make some slight acquaintances. You still get walked past.

You decide the school gate is a hostile environment. They're all on their guard. There's nothing wrong with you. It just takes time, that's human nature. You'd better ask Kirsty or Emma or Justin to tea tomorrow.

You'd also better stop being concerned. Why should you care? Stop wanting to be liked. Just do what you gotta do. Then you might find you can casually exchange the time of day, crack a joke and move on. Or tomorrow, when you go to collect the kids, take a book to read.

There are other puzzles. These just have to be their husbands' company cars; in which case do *all* the husbands go to work on the train? And how is it that the thin ones are all as smart as pins in their long leather boots and Fiorucci jeans and make-up at 8.45 a.m.? Perhaps they prepare themselves at night and lie down carefully between some chocks.

Eventually you get involved with other mothers because you share lifts. In the morning as you sit amid the breakfast things with your diary and your lists you decide whether collecting children today clashes with your hair appointment and whether Joan or Pru could collect them. And if so can they give them tea in which case they will be OK until six o'clock and you can get some work done *and* pop into the garden centre! Or

whether it should be all done in reverse, i.e. you have them to
tea.

Sometimes to your surprise you find you can get on just fine
with one or two mothers. Both of you are straightforward and
practical and friendly, there are no overtones or undertones,
neither of you worries about who owes whom. It almost leads
you to think you can have an actual friendship with a woman.

Popping in for coffee

You don't realise, until you're a housewife, just how much
popping in for coffee goes on. Then you find that it goes on
everywhere all the time, like wave motion in the sea which
propels a surge of tiny denizens and crablets in one direction
and next moment has them all pouring back again to a slightly
different place.

In fact popping in for coffee is the nation's intelligence
system. Popping in for coffee means freedom, quality of life,
free speech, citizen's rights. No one takes this away from us.
Important news can be round the nation in the space of a few
cups.

But how do you, a man, get in on this? Once you used to
have your morning coffee at work. If you were important your
secretary brought it on a tray in a cup and saucer with some
biscuits. If you were like the rest of us you got it from the
machine. But here you are today. You've cleared up the
breakfast things, looked in the cupboard, made a list, sewn a
button on, cut it off again because it wouldn't go through the
buttonhole. You're a bit bored. You've tried running round the
house with no clothes on singing the Ode to Joy from the
Choral Symphony while you were putting the laundry away.
Then the milkman came up the drive while you were prancing
about and you had to hide under the table.

You get dressed again and you sit in the kitchen. You

wonder whether you want another cup of coffee already. Then the phone rings.

'Hello,' it says. 'Is that you, Jill?'

'No,' you say. 'Jill is out at work.'

'Oh, of course,' it says. 'I forgot. This is Jane.'

'Hello,' you say. 'Can I take a message?'

'No,' she says. 'Not really. I was just going out and I wondered if I could pop in and collect Tricia's tracksuit top as I go past.'

'Of course,' you say. 'I didn't know she'd left it. Any time.'

'In about half an hour?'

'Fine.'

'Bye, then.'

Suddenly the morning has purpose. Jane is calling to collect a tracksuit top. A thought enters your mind. Surely she knows Jill goes to work by now? You dismiss it. Are there any biscuits left? You put the kettle on. You wipe the table. You begin to sweep the floor. There is a knock at the door.

'Hello,' you say. 'Come in.'

'Thanks,' she says. 'Sorry to be such a nuisance. Ah, there it is. She has gym today as well.'

'Stay and have a cup of coffee,' you say.

'Oh, no, I mustn't,' she says.

'Have a quick cup,' you say. 'It's all ready.'

'All right, but very quick. I really mustn't stay.'

At last: you are in. Someone has popped in for coffee. You wouldn't think so from the preceding dialogue, but it is so. You could be forgiven for thinking that your visitor is in a terrific hurry and very busy and feels guilty about permitting herself to stop for coffee and a chat.

You can then say, for example:

'Should we have real coffee for a treat?'

'Oh, no, instant will do for me.'

Note the modest self-denial. You make some real coffee.

'Wonderful coffee,' your visitor murmurs. She looks around the kitchen. Don't be so misguided as to serve the coffee in the sitting room. It's cold and formal in the morning. Coffee in the mornings should be taken either in the kitchen or in bed.

'How tidy and well organised you are!' she says, awakening you from your mental picture of coffee in bed.

'Oh, not particularly,' you say with statutory self-deprecation. 'But one has to do one's bit.'

'Jill is *so* lucky. Dennis hardly ever does a thing.' She sighs. 'But he is terribly busy these days.'

Poor sod, you think. He doesn't even know whether the sun is shining this morning.

'How is Dennis getting on?' you ask.

'Awfully well, really. He took over the whole of the Southern Region last month.'

You glance out of the window. So that's why you didn't recognise the car.

'Well, I must be going,' she says. 'How are the children? Thank you for the *lovely* coffee.'

'Very well, thank you. That's all right,' you say.

At this stage she may or may not say: 'Do pop in for coffee next time you're passing. It's so nice to have a chat.'

It's more probable that she won't. This is because you're a man and the odds are against her Inviting a Man. If you are desperate to pop in, etc. you present yourself on the doorstep, and say you think your daughter left her tracksuit bottom here by mistake.

If, of course, you develop genuine friendship or neighbourly intimacy with other ladies, then the conversation over coffee is very different. Then you can just pop in, or pop round. The conversation goes something like this. You open the back door and call:

'Yoo hoo!'

Voice from upstairs: 'Cooee. Come in. With you in a minute.'

You come in, walk around a bit, stare at their things lying round, finger the morning's post on the table and put the kettle on.

The neighbour appears, straightening her skirt. No make-up on. This must be a real pal. Perhaps she sees you as another woman. Perhaps you have dressed up as one so you can really integrate.

'Hello,' she says. 'Excuse the mess.'

'I was just passing,' you say.

'Here,' she says. 'Have you talked to Pauline recently?'

'Not for a week,' you say.

'Oh,' she says. 'You won't have heard. They're not getting on at all well.'

Ah, you think. This is more like it. 'Really?' you say. 'You mean Pauline and Geoff? I thought they had patched things up.'

'No!' she replies scornfully. 'Not Pauline and Geoff! They reached an understanding a long time ago. That was before her mother came to stay and before Tom had his accident. No! It's not Pauline and Geoff! It's Pauline and Alan!'

You gaze at her open-mouthed. Who is Alan? What was the understanding? Is her mother still there? What was Tom's accident? What happened with Geoff? For that matter, who is Pauline?

Your mind whirls with unspoken questions. You know now that you will come back again and again and – pop in for coffee.

Sales parties

If you are a terribly successful housewife and really look the part, and what's more, if your wife allows you some spare money, you may be invited to sales parties. You need to know what to do; how to behave; whether to buy anything. The originals of all such parties seem to have been the well-known Scupperware parties. You go for a coffee and another chat at somebody's house. You come away with armfuls of totally

Things you can buy at sales parties

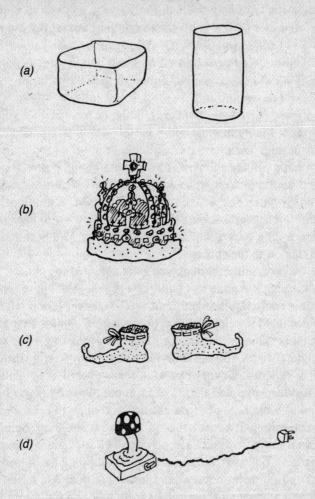

(a)

(b)

(c)

(d)

useless but terribly useful plastic containers and picnic plates and travelling tea sets. When you get home you put them on the table and gaze at them in fury. You can give that one to Grandma and those to Auntie Sheila and the long one to the church jumble. Then you wrap them up again and put them in the bottom drawer where their fate is to accumulate.

The economics of such parties are cloaked in genteel obscurity. Are you slowly enriching your neighbour? Is it rude to refuse to go? Or is it rude to ask you? Perhaps if you drink a lot of coffee you won't be asked again because you are too expensive. You can always reflect that you are supporting the nation's hidden economy. If they go to Mallorca again you know you overdid it.

These parties are, of course, designed for women. Coffee is served. Light chit-chat and repartee, slowly the tension is mounting. Then, pow! The hostess brings the goodies in. Or perhaps you are all taken into the next room. Where are you this morning? You are at a jewellery party. A little something for the wife? You hesitate. You are shy. Oh, come along! they shrill, what sort of thing does she like? You try to explain that you want a ruby and pair of tassels set like Mrs Forbes is trying on in the corner.

Or on another morning you have collected the child allowance and gone to a children's clothes sale. Quite good value really. Does anything fit you? You need a new left sock since the dog helped you sort the washing. Isn't it strange how mothers know what size their children are? Bring a few vests home anyway. You can always stretch them by wearing them yourself for a day. Or they can go in the cupboard along with the salad dispenser and the set of El Topaz Moroccan ankle bangles.

But something new and exciting is coming to housewives' sales parties. It's hardly begun. It sounds shocking. Surely, you'd think, it's much too private? The latest thing is sex aid parties. Yes, after the coffee and biscuits are over, it's no holds barred – fearless housewives confronting their real selves. You can't go to one of these parties in trousers. If you want to take the risk and go disguised as your wife, well, on your head be it.

If you don't know what sex aids are, don't worry, nobody else did until Mrs Kerthorpe's coffee morning last week. Now everybody does except you. Perhaps someone will tell you if you play your cards right.

Keeping the house clean enough for the cleaning lady

If you're a man and relatively inexperienced in these matters, one of the great household paradoxes is the function of the cleaning lady. If your wife didn't tell you, you'll soon find out. Sometimes you will hear a woman say:

'I must tidy up, I've got the cleaning lady coming.'

On the face of it this is a surprising statement. It has a number of variants, such as:

'I'll just clean the cooker, then Dora can really get on.'

Or: 'I can't let Mrs Hernandez find the bedroom in this state.'

The last one gives a bit of the game away. Women want to have the housework done but they don't want it to be thought that they're *too* mucky or untidy. They shouldn't worry. Cleaning ladies can read the signs. They know exactly how mucky and untidy you are.

There is a bigger mystery from a man's simplistic point of view. Do cleaning ladies clean? 'I thought we paid her,' you say naïvely to your wife. 'Why didn't she clean inside the cooker as well?'

'Because it's a nasty, filthy job,' your wife says. 'We can't expect Mrs Threlfall-Smyth to do it. That's your job.'

Well, you think; marketplace economics being tempered by the caring society. But you're lucky. Not everyone can afford a cleaning lady. Or if they can, not everyone can find one.

It depends where you live. Friends of ours advertised when times were hard. They got thirty applicants and had to have a short list and interviews. They finished up with a paragon. To be precise the paragon interviewed them. She was very efficient and stacked socks in drawers. The family were very clean but intimidated and hardly dared get out of bed – or still less into it.

That's what happens if you go beyond the happy medium.

Don't help the cleaning lady make the beds

Let your cleaning lady clean so far and no further. Remember that even good things are only good up to a point.

Suppose you are at home one morning. The cleaning lady comes. If she is new she will be quite surprised to find you there. She will be even more surprised if you start wandering round getting in her way whistling and pretending to dust or tidy things. So don't. Let her get on with it. Pretend you're a professional person working from home this morning, not a male skivvy.

It will be OK to offer her coffee or a cup of tea. You can have a nice chat. If she cleans for other people you know she will either be the soul of discretion about them or not. If not, pretend to be only moderately interested, because if you now know about the state of their cupboards and drawers, they will know about yours.

After you've finished coffee and she says she must do the upstairs now, don't volunteer to help her make the beds. She will probably think you're just like her hubby and men are all the same.

If the cleaning lady isn't coming and nobody pops in for coffee this morning you can chat to the milkman, once he has got over his surprise or disappointment at seeing who it is. Milkmen nearly always are friendly and chatty. If it's an icy morning or near Christmas the thing to do is offer him a nip. If it's warm you can go out and lean on the gate. Idly you watch your dog biting the wheels of the milk float as it retreats up the road.

What a pleasure to lean on the gate on a fine morning. Sniff the air. Wave to Mrs Thing. Wipe your hands on your apron. Through the open door the smell of fresh coffee drifts. Music on the radio half-heard. The robin hops on the fence nearby. Your poor wife, you think. Off in the hurly-burly again. Her life rushing by.

Lines begin to form in your head.

POEM

This morning, leaning on the garden gate,
How idly you could watch the world outside,
Reflecting safely on the rush-hour tide
And waving to the lingerers, and the late.
How snugly, smugly then you might turn round.
– But suddenly you felt the gate's hard edge,
You heard the robin scratching in the hedge,
You saw the moss-grown pebble on the ground,
And smelt a wisp of biting bonfire smoke.
. . . You knew the morning's presence in the air
And saw, because another sense awoke,
Yourself, as if a stranger, standing there.
The inner and the outer worlds are one;
But even as you look, the moment's gone.

You rush into the house to write down your poem. Blow the housework. And what the neighbours think.

8
Sex
or
How to have your cake

THIS IS where it all comes OK.

The comfort, the refreshment, the joy of marriage. Closeness, warmth, trust. Tears, teasing – and fun.

It is evening. The curtains are drawn. Your home is warm and cosy. The children have had their supper and are doing their clay modelling or their tapestry.

'Time for bed, children,' you murmur. Obediently they put their things away neatly and trot upstairs, kissing you on the way.

You look at your watch. Half-past seven already! You meant to have a bath and change before Hermione (your wife) gets home. She might be home any minute. You dash upstairs, run the razor over your chin, dash on a little Monsieur Fleuri and loosely knot a Pierre Lemerdeux scarf round your neck. You rush down again and lay the table. Another hour passes.

Presently you hear your wife at the door. You run and open it for her.

'Hello, Herm,' you say softly.

'What's for dinner?' she asks, glancing past you into the kitchen. She sniffs. 'What's the smell?' she says.

'It's just my aftershave, darling,' you answer, 'mixing with the garlic in the dinner.'

You sit down to eat. There is silence for a while as two tired, hungry people slowly unwind. Your wife is reading the newspaper.

'Had a good day at the office, dear?' you inquire brightly.

'What?' your wife replies. 'Oh. Er. Lousy.'

Silence falls again. You bite your lip. Was it always like this? What happened to the carefree, attractive girl you married? Suddenly it all wells over and you burst out bitterly:

'The children are asleep and you haven't even kissed them goodnight!'

If this doesn't apply, or for a change, you can burst out bitterly:

'You never get home early any more and my hotpot's ruined!'

Your wife doesn't reply. She is getting philosophical too. What is there to say? You relent.

'You go and watch television, dear,' you say. 'I'll bring you some coffee.'

'All right,' she says, getting up. 'And bring the whisky, would you?'

You sigh. It can't be good for her, sitting in front of the TV sipping whisky. And yet . . . if it cheers her up a little . . .

The evening passes. You busy yourself with a little mending. Your wife is snoozing in front of a repeat of the *Money Programme*. You seem to be drifting further and further apart.

Suddenly you are dog tired. 'I'm off to bed,' you announce. Upstairs you step woodenly out of your clothes. You catch a glimpse of yourself in the mirror. Sagging, lined, old. You climb into bed. You don't even bother to take off your aftershave. You turn out the light, pull the pillow over your ears and close your eyes.

Some time later you half-hear the door open and your wife stumbles in.

'Why is this b***** light always off?' you hear her mutter. Now she is undressing. You hear the frou-frou of the silk as the Janet Reger cami-bodice is drawn over her head. Then a bump and a grunt as she gets into bed. Silence falls.

Involuntarily, your mind goes back to earlier days, when you used to lie on one elbow watching your wife undress, a Chopin nocturne playing on the gramophone. How eagerly you watched then as she drew her dress off over her head. Oh, there was no silk in those days. Heavy-duty knickers, woolly vests, what did it matter? Impatiently you would wait for the taut curve of her breast to appear. Hungrily your eye ran down the flat belly to the tufted shadow beneath. And now . . . you clench your teeth in your sleep and pull the pillow tighter round your head.

Suddenly you are wide awake. Under the bedclothes a hand has touched you. It is on your hip. It advances. You lie still. If you pretend to be asleep perhaps it will go away. No. It advances resolutely. Suddenly it delves – and grasps!

Panic seizes you. What should you do? You wrench yourself free and turn away. You stare into the darkness. What should you say? You hardly recognise the strangled voice as your own.

'Not tonight, dear. I'm having one of my headaches.'

Getting it together

What went wrong? Perhaps you have been taking your household duties too seriously. Perhaps you have become tense and anxious. Unsympathetic and unreceptive: it's no good being a good housekeeper (or even a bad one) if this is the result.

Let's try something different.

Years ago we had one of those books called *Advice to Young People Considering Marriage* or *So You're Going to Get Married?* It was mostly concerned with the duties of the best man or what goes in the bottom drawer. But it contained one chapter with the remarkable title of 'Fire in the Bedroom'. You could be forgiven for thinking it was about coal-burning grates or the risks of smoking in bed. No, it was about shyness, modesty and respect. It ended with a poem about daffodils and crocuses peeping up.

So what are you going to do to restore the rapture? Smoke in bed? Be shy and modest? Keep a volume of *Great Moments from Gardeners' Question Time* by the bedside?

You can do better than that. Now that your wife is out at work and comes home tired, now that you are running the home, you must secretly prepare yourself for those careless moments of intimacy. It isn't enough to open the door to your wife wearing a frilly apron in front and a feather duster behind. It isn't enough to buy her a box of chocolates the day after she said you didn't care about her any more and you threw the frying pan down the garden path and said she was just like her mother.

You must become a more complete person. Accomplish your basic household tasks. Remember your quirky off-beat humour at awkward moments. And brush up those little basic skills you have neglected for so long or thought you wouldn't need again after you left school.

Technique

You thought you knew all there was to know about technique. Well, you were wrong. How wrong you were. But stay calm and read on.

Foreplay. This is something which in some sports is called knocking up. Now you know why. Foreplay, or FP as we like to call it out of Victorian prudery, is when you lovingly arouse your partner. Holding the alarm clock to their ear is a good way of lovingly arousing most partners. FP should continue until your partner indicates by affectionate signs that she is ready. If FP has gone on for a fortnight you should break off for a cup of tea. She will have gone off the boil by then.

Four-play. This is when Scrabble with the neighbours runs off the board. As usual, you get left with the X (eight points).

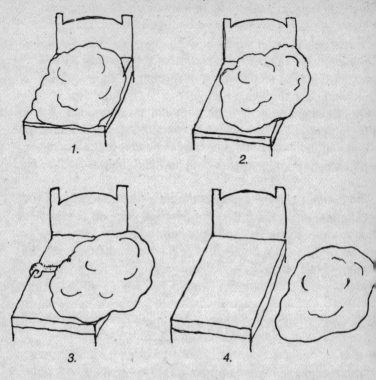

Press-ups. You always hated press-ups. This is your chance to enjoy them.

Turkish porter's lift. This is a very useful technique indeed. It enables you to carry on with the housework and do other things at the same time. In the old days it used to save the porters getting slipped discs while humping things in the bazaar. You may need to practise a little before you can get round the dusting as quickly as usual. Note that if you bend down you may not be able to get up again. This technique can also be carried into the garden, and in theory it enables you to go shopping, but this is not advisable in some areas.

Cartwheels. Cartwheels may not be for you as they are excruciatingly painful and uncomfortable. Once you are through the pain barrier there is the satisfaction of technical achievement. This technique is conducted on the front lawn.

The 'look, no hands'. A technique for the daredevil. Careful you don't crash into the furniture.

The chandelier. This legendary technique requires space. Now you know why all your neighbours are having extensions built. It also requires ceiling height, but failing this you can excavate a parabolic groove in the floor.

The vacuum cleaner. Ideal for the man about the house. Calls for combination of technical skill, manual dexterity, physical courage, brute strength, excellent balance and impeccable manners. Your wife should also have an iron constitution, nerves of steel and impeccable manners. Remember to have the vacuum serviced regularly.

That little selection should keep you busy. You may like to save some of them up for treats on special days like your wedding anniversary or April Fool's Day. Once a year is quite enough for most of them anyway.

Aphrodisiac food

A man can transform a marriage utterly by his skills in the kitchen. Now you have it in your power to serve up a variety of ravishing concoctions, see if you can really surprise your wife by the strange new impulses she feels after eating your food.

Here are some suggestions for ingenious delicacies. Remember that it's easier to seduce a woman in the kitchen than in any other room in the house. Have her sit there and watch while you prepare something special for her.

Paella 'el blotto'. This pungent mound of variegated rice combined with blobs of saffron, undecorticated shrimps and slices of banana will start off by reminding your wife irresistibly of that holiday in Alicante where you stayed in a hotel with a bright yellow bathroom. After a while she will be obliged to go upstairs and lie down until the gripes pass off. After a decent interval you tiptoe upstairs and find her in bed fully dressed and fast asleep. You try waking her but she pushes you away muttering:

'Gerroff, Pablo!'

You ponder the meaning of this as you fall asleep.

Rude spaghetti. This is an immensely painstaking dish to prepare. But an accomplished kitchen expert such as you, and particularly one intent on making a fond overture to his wife, will find the time and patience to tackle it. You buy a tin of alphabet spaghetti and warm it up. Spaghetti is a yellowish-orange sort of colour, so you need a contrasting shade to go with it. A pack of frozen spinach is ideal. You warm this up too. You serve the dish with random spaghetti round the side and a flat bed of spinach in the middle. Clearly legible on the spinach, written in spaghetti, are the words:

HOW ABOUT IT TONITE

You smile affectionately. Your wife's head is bent over her plate as she reads her dinner. Is she eating it? No, she is fiddling about with it. A reply! Something tender and intimate, no doubt. She pushes the plate over to you. It says:

HATE COLD SPAGHETTI

Toad in the hole. You used to think this was a kid's dish. Oh, no. Not since Freud. Just like you can't make films of trains

(a) A magnificent show of
    toad in the hole

(b) A delicate serving of
    prime parsnips with
    butter

(c) A late-night snack of
    fibre-rich frozen peas
    sprinkled with
    ginseng, with a
    dramatic fish finger as
    a saucy symbol of
    promise

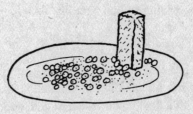

(d) Appetising portions of
    mashed potatoes with
    gin

going into tunnels for children any more, so you can't make toad in the hole for kids. The blatant symbolism of it: the womb-like batter; the toad – I mean, the sausage – nestling there as you stick your fork into the brown, nicely rounded outside. Offer it shyly to your wife. Be very gentle.

Parsnips. It's not generally recognised what a potent effect a large plate of parsnips can have. Choose the biggest, knobbliest parsnips you can find. Don't forget to cook them. When tender serve with lashings of butter. Some people prefer to keep the lashings and the butter separate.

While your partner is eating the parsnips observe her closely. Nibble at a little yourself meanwhile. Beware of eating too much too quickly in case you lose control. When she begins to blink and have difficulty swallowing, this is the moment for you to thrust the parsnips, and the butter, aside and move in smoothly.

You may have to carry her upstairs, or out into the garden, according to how you like to respond to moments of peak living.

Lychees. Lychees are those squishy pale round fruits you can order for pudding in Chinese restaurants. Now you know why you get so few of them. Their unpredictable effect on women must be based on sympathetic magic, i.e. because they remind them of squishy pale round fruits.

Ginseng. Famous all-purpose substance from the East. Can be sprinkled on anything. Washes off easily. You can also make ginseng tea. Good for eyes, ears, nose, throat, hands, feet, hair, skin, navel, digestion and morale, so probably good for you-know-what too. Can be given to cats, dogs and children.

Avocado pear. Tell wife to go to bed. Take large ripe avocado, cut in half, throw pip at dog. Make delectable garlicky vinaigrette, pour into holes in avocado. Take upstairs and eat in bed. Lick up drips.

Alcohol. Your old friend. A little alcohol, as you know, works wonders with a girl's defences. But be subtle. You are an artist. You are preparing a delicate, seductive supper. The aim is to introduce a little inebriation into the menu without it being noticed. Here are some practical ideas.

Mashed potatoes with gin. Stir quite a lot of gin into the mashed potatoes. When the loved one remarks that they taste funny, say that you have added a few crushed juniper berries.

Whisky stuffing. When preparing the sage and onion stuffing for your chicken, dilute the stuffing mix with whisky instead of water. This will enliven your old bird all right.

Rum custard. This is a variant on brandy sauce. Buy a small Christmas pudding, make some custard, pour in half a bottle of rum. Explain that the pudding has matured.

Vodka toast. Make some toast, soak in vodka. Pour cold baked beans on top and serve as a tasty pre-theatre snack.

So much for food. Now for something really serious.

High-risk scenarios with the opposite sex

You have packed your wife off to catch her train. Or maybe she has burbled off up the road in the BMW. The children are at school. You have cleared up the breakfast things, swept the floor, wormed the cat, been to the shop to buy half a pound of Meat Heap for supper.

Now you are at the Mother's Fellowship coffee morning in aid of a mini-computer for the infants school. The vicar's wife asked you to go specially, they like your company and as you were a man you could tell them about computers!

So you hold your cup and saucer and piece of homemade shortbread and chat. You glance back at a pair of eyes a little

Hello! Some coffee?

Try some of my dip . . .

Do buy a raffle ticket!

That's all right. It was only my toe/knee/elbow/nipple

way away. You look again. No, it's not an accident. She is looking at you.

What do her eyes say exactly?

Your mind goes back to that party in 1979, or was it '69? Or was it the gallery preview? No, it was the Yashmak Perfumes product launch. The brown eyes over the top of the wine glass. The immediate rapport. Her gaze on your face. The breathlessness, the nervousness in the stomach. Her hand near yours. The tingling of energy on your skin. The knowledge of her desires.

. . . You come back to the present. You are at the coffee morning, a woman is looking at you. She is coming closer. She speaks.

'Another cup of coffee?' She smiles.

'Oh!' you say. 'Just half a cup. Very nice coffee. Thank you.'

'Aren't we lucky with the weather?' she chirps as she takes your cup.

So much for your sultry gaze. Get on the wavelength, you say to yourself, understand what is going on. From across the room a powerful stare is directed at you. It is the ex-president but three of the Women's Institute. She spends her pension on rum. She is very, very tough.

'So!' she booms. 'The only man here, eh? Keeps you busy, doesn't it? Have you contributed yet?'

You answer these various propositions with a loud nod. You are rescued by the vicar's wife. She pats your arm. Her compassionate eyes blink at you.

'Do tell us about computers! The computer will be marvellous for the children, won't it? What kind of things will they be able to do with it?'

You consider saying that they could run the school stock control system on it or enter all their marks so you could actually find out if your kid is brighter or dimmer than the others. Finally you say that computers are wonderful for training children in disciplined thinking and quick responses. Especially, you add as an afterthought, if you buy them Asteroids and Gobblers.

The vicar's wife frowns slightly. She pats your arm again.

'They're so clever nowadays, aren't they? Well, I must go and help in the kitchen now.'

The coffee morning draws to a close. You eat another vol-au-vent and doze peacefully on your feet. But it may not be like this every time. Unwittingly, unwillingly, you may find yourself caught up in a tricky scenario. That'll teach you not to read the signals properly. Yes, we know you meant well. You were only going to tell her about a homeopathic doctor, or about a little man who welds up Morris Minors.

The white wine scenario. This risk situation occurs behind the scenes at ladies' mornings and luncheons. Because you are a man you are asked to help with the wine. This is an outmoded sexist concept but you agree anyway. In the kitchen you strike up a working relationship with the girl who in theory can't pull corks. You both get tiddly and get in each other's way on purpose all the time. Finally you both can't stand it any longer and you are having a passionate kiss when the door opens and someone comes in to get a tea towel. Muttering apologies the person retreats immediately so you never know who saw you.

The mince pie scenario. This predicament can be deceptively pleasant. It is the situation offering the quickest cycle between awakened curiosity and repletion, not to say distaste.

It may be at a party. It may be Christmas, which gives rise to a prevalence of mince pies and an ambivalence of merriment. You are, so to speak, closeted with a woman. She may have cornered you with a plate of mince pies. You may have been creeping away round the back of the sofa when she cut you off. Or again you may have been inveigled into the kitchen to help with things.

She looks up at you. Her eyes shine with enthusiasm and a little sherry. You think to yourself that actually she is quite pretty. Sometimes your kids play with hers. Her husband and you once had a drink together.

'These mince pies are absolutely mmmh!' she declares. The last word is a glottal phoneme with labial restriction followed by a nasal plosive. Otherwise known as a socially refined grunt.

'Are they?' you reply. 'I haven't had one yet.' Fool. Utter fool. You asked for it and you got it.

'Haven't you?' she says. 'Here you are . . . open wide!' Politely you open your mouth. She pops a mince pie into it. You close your mouth. The two of you gaze at each other while you chew. She puts her head a little on one side.

'Nice?' she asks.

'Lovely, thank you.' You cough on a crumb and sip some wine.

'Aren't you going to offer me one?' she murmurs.

Momentarily you hesitate. The wine has gone to your head. What is she really inviting you to do? You pick up a mince pie. She opens her mouth slightly. You advance the mince pie. She opens her mouth a bit more. You try to glance round the room without moving your head or eyes. Finally you put the mince pie in her mouth. She has some fillings. Her lips brush your fingers.

At this point any of a number of things will happen:

(a) She will offer you another mince pie, and so on *ad nauseam*.

(b) One of you will put the mince pies to one side and say decisively

> *either*: (i) 'This is foolishness; let's be lovers.'
> *or*: (ii) 'This is foolishness; let's go back to the others.'

If you're slightly deaf try to be sure which she said, or if you're slightly drunk try to be sure which you said.

(c) Her husband will turn up saying, 'I thought we were going.'

(d) The hostess will turn up saying, 'Oh good. You two are still here.'

Whatever happens, thereafter you will feel differently about mince pies.

The startled faun scenario. This is an exceptionally difficult situation to deal with and, indeed, one which could lead to arrest and disgrace if you are unlucky.

You are just easing your way behind Mrs Mossibank at a crowded party, murmuring 'Excuse me' inaudibly, when she leaps in the air and spins round.

'Oh! Charles!' she cries. 'You are a one!'

People smile tolerantly. She puts her hands on yours or wherever.

'You shouldn't do that sort of thing.' She drops her voice. 'But it was nice.'

The correct course is to take no notice of this at all. The cardinal error is to think that next time you can or should touch her. Anyway, next time you pass you put both hands on her waist from behind.

If you're lucky she will merely leap in the air again with a terrible giggle. She is ticklish or pretends to be. If you're unlucky she will whirl round with a howl of pleasure and grapple with you.

Creep away, give her a wide berth and prepare for the most alarming eventuality of all.

The predatory female scenario. You aren't at a party or in the village hall or somewhere innocent like that. You are at her house. Mind you, in all innocence you have come round to put up a shelf or fix a dripping tap. Because she asked you.

You turn up with your tool box. She shows you where she wants the shelf. In fact she goes on showing you. She passes you things and says how kind it is. With so much help it takes quite a long time to get the shelf up. You have to drill several holes very close to each other and it still doesn't look quite level. Your friend says it is just fine and can you put things on it right away. You deck the shelf out and step back to admire it. This is where you make your mistake. You take your eyes off her.

Suddenly, like a panther pouncing on its puny prey, with one bound she is on you. Locked together you both roll over and over. Every time she is on top you hear your ribs crack.

What should you do? Hit her on the back of the head with an ivory statuette? Prefer death to dishonour (most unlike you) and tip the piano over on you both?

You feel dizzy. It is getting hard to breathe. Desperately you look around. The window is open.

'Samantha,' you grit into her ear. 'I give up.'

'Darling,' she purrs. 'I knew you would. Let's make beautiful music together.'

She relaxes her grip. Quick as a flash you hurl yourself out of the window and into the flower bed. You pick yourself up and run for your life.

How you get your tool box back is your problem.

9
The masculine touch

or

What makes a home?

THERE ARE many little things the man about the house can do to show what a good housekeeper he is, and to make a home a home. When your wife gets home, when the neighbours call, when the children come romping in, it's those special touches which make the difference. They make the family feel secure and loved, and visitors welcome and at ease.

A little skill helps with these things, but often it's the thought behind the action – a man taking trouble, a man giving a little of himself to others.

For example, does your wife ever come home to a vase of spring flowers on the table? The dog to a freshly laundered blanket? The children to a tube of Smarties by their plates?

Here are some things you can do.

Flower arranging

This lovely art can be yours with a little time and trouble. Of all skills and pastimes, flower arrangement can most readily bring beauty and joy into the home.

Beauty is in the flowers, but beauty in the arrangement springs from the goodwill the arranger brings to it. You need to prepare yourself a little before arranging flowers. You add to the flowers the harmony and balance you have in yourself.

This sounds very serious and so it is. Fortunately we are also able to bring to your help a series of detailed drawings which

Flower arrangements for men

(a) Basic principles

1 Balance

Balance is the first consideration. If you have a big flower on one side, have little ones on the other

2 Colour

Use colour in clever combinations and contrasts

3 Harmony

Select your flowers according to shape and family to achieve overall integration

4 Space

Don't crowd your settings. Allow space and light to play their part

5 The vase

Pick a beautiful container to reflect the spirit of your flowers

6 Foliage

Allow the natural spread of leaves to assist the effect

(b) Special settings

1 A spring arrangement

2 A winter arrangement

3 A bouquet for a dear friend

4 A setting for a dinner table

5 A sensitive arrangement

6 An oriental arrangement

1 Morning glory
Wonderful in the corner of the loo.
Attach to wall with sticky tape

2 Pampas
Grass in a bucket. Very evocative
of the hot wastelands. Don't
overwater

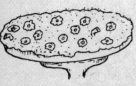

3 A Midsummer Night's Dream
Daisies on a bed of moss. Good for
stubbing out cigarettes. Fits on little
round tables

4 Tiger, tiger . . .
Thrilling tableau of the Burmese
jungle. Set up on a tea tray. How
you get cat to stay there is your
problem. Try glue

5 The fountains of Rome
Exciting yet peaceful aquatic
ambiance for floating flowers and
wild life

6 The hills are loud . . .
Majestic Alpine setting for your
rockery flowers and Auntie's cactus.
Build with old bricks and hard core
on sitting-room carpet for maximum
effect

take you quickly from first principles to advanced flower settings. Very quickly. You can also go to classes in flower arrangement with other housewives. But this depends on whether your wife will babysit while you go out.

So off you go into the garden. It's a fine morning. You've opened the windows to air the house. What would be nicer than to put some flowers in different rooms? Flowers immediately bring nature into the house. They present to the eye the miraculous shapes and colours of the real world. They embalm the air.

What have you got in the garden? Not much? What about the neighbours? Perhaps you could borrow some flowers. Or perhaps you'd better go for a walk in the park. Or along the hedgerows.

Somewhere you can find some flowers. Even if you have to buy them. What you have to work with depends on the season, of course.

So you bring your flowers in. You have brought some foliage too, or branches or grasses. Spread them all out on the kitchen table. This is a wonderful moment. Enjoy your flowers. Touch them, speak to them. The flowers themselves will begin to define how you arrange them, by their shape, colour, compatibility. You may want to shorten stems or divide branches. In a strange way it doesn't matter how you arrange them as long as you work towards balance, harmony, harmonious contrast, appropriateness.

Naturally, if you went to a class, there would be rules of arrangement. If you studied with an eastern master of flower arrangement, you would also find rules – but philosophical rules in the first instance.

But enough of philosophy. Here is a selection of flower settings to brighten the house, soften your wife's heart, instil a sense of wonder in your children and earn the admiration of visitors.

In the kitchen. Here, where you spend so much time, you want fruity, hedgerow arrangements, or bunches of herbs hanging from hooks. The bounty of nature should be your theme. When you come back from the greengrocer, put out your apples and veg in bowls or in an open basket if you have one.

In the living room. Here you want flowers of the season. In spring, so many bright yellow flowers bringing in new light: daffodils, iris, sprays of forsythia. As the season advances, bring in all that is fresh and new: hawthorn blossom, lilac, lupins, sweet peas. And, in autumn, the divinely mellow chrysanthemum.

In the hall. Here you may want something more arresting. You should move the rampant but rotting rubber plant you brought from your office. Stop wasting milk on it. Put it in the bath. In the hall we suggest an extravagant display of exotica. If you have a pickaxe or a hammer drill, make a hole in the floor and plant a vine. In a few years' time you will be able to greet your guests under a veritable bower of Dionysos. On a more modest scale you should go for something like the Malayan flowering beetroot. This puts forth attractive purple tendrils and exudes a drowsy perfume, but take care it doesn't eat the cat.

In the bedroom. Ah! Here you should blend your art with nature's to create an other-worldly but delicately suggestive atmosphere. Fill the room with the heady scent of honeysuckle. Or on a summer's evening when the windows have been open all day and you have freshly made the bed with grandmother's embroidered cambric sheets, lay on the dear one's pillow . . . one perfect rose. If you haven't got a rose, don't make the mistake of substituting something less or making a humorous gesture such as putting a leek or a fried egg on her pillow. She may chuckle or even thank you but in her heart of hearts she will think you are fundamentally a silly person.

In the lavatory. Here you need a rather strong arrangement and we suggest a thoughtful composition of rhubarb. There is a certain sombre beauty in the great leaves as they unfold massively from the bucket in the corner. Rhubarb will readily absorb the faintest tinge of malodour and the leaves are soft and strong in case of emergency. Add plenty of sugar when you make rhubarb pie later.

A welcoming fire

There is nothing like an open fire to create real warmth and a homely atmosphere: the firelight glinting off the cups on the dresser, the cat sitting blinking at the flames, the children's eyes shining as you read them their goodnight story. And later, after supper, you and she sitting in front of the flickering embers. She with her mug of cocoa, you with your mug of brandy. And then up to bed.

What a pity you took the fireplace out last year. Why don't you poke through the plasterboard and see if you can take that out as well.

But if you have a fireplace and the weather is chilly, why wait? Get some logs – much more romantic than coal – and a packet of firelighters. If your fire smokes, it may be because the logs are damp. Don't worry, they dry out while burning. When they've practically burnt away they hardly smoke at all. The other thing you can do if the fire smokes is open all the doors to make a draught and put your coat on.

Firelight is so attractive, isn't it? If you turn the lights down to create a cosy twilight, you'll find you can't see the dust and the grime any more. So if your wife's coming home late and you haven't cleaned the place up, take the bulb out of the ceiling light.

Clever hands

If your wife isn't back yet, and you're sitting on your own, and time hangs heavily, what can you do? Time was when you would have put up a shelf, or repaired a radio, or replaced the washer in the bathroom tap. But of course your wife does that

Things a man can knit or embroider

1. Family crest on wife's knickers

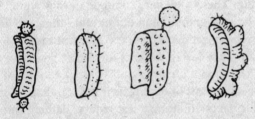

2. Different models of woolly cover for teapot handles

3. Woolly lavatory seat sleeve for cold mornings, with inspiring biblical text

sort of thing now. And she has taken the car, so you can't check the levels or charge the battery, and anyway she will see to all that at the weekend. What is there that's satisfying and creative?

You can monogram all the towels, for a start. Begin with your initials and then go on to the family crest. It might be well worth inventing a coat of arms if you don't happen to have one. Think of future generations. A family motto is also necessary, preferably in Latin. Examples:

Per ardua ad uxorem.
Non Ford sed Rolls-Royce me movebit.

You can think up more while you work at your embroidery. After doing the towels you can go on to the sheets, the tea towels and the family's underwear. The children will be so proud during gym lessons.

A very useful thing a man can do, if his knitting is just the teeniest bit limited, is to knit woolly covers for teapot handles. See drawing. These were very common during World War II, probably because grannies ran out of other things to do. If these are all you can make, don't worry, just make a lot of them. They make lovely presents for people who have everything.

Then there are lots of other things you can knit. Tom Kitten trousers for the cat. Lavatory seat covers. Bathing costumes – always a good laugh the first time someone goes for a swim in a knitted one.

A little drinks party

Now you've got your house just so, clean, tidy, well appointed, unusual flower arrangements and knitted dingly-dangles in every room, you must do some entertaining. Some of your friends don't believe you actually do all those things, like cook

Interesting snacks to make for a drinks party

1. *Oignons au diable. Onion outsides stuffed with sausage meat*

2. *Scotch onions. Onion insides rolled in clever sausage meat jacket*

3. *Dessert onions. Serve as a surprise sweetmeat. Garnish with honey and cooking chocolate*

4. *A dip. Make plenty while you're at it. Don't cut the celery too short.*
   Ingredients of dip: 2 pints mayonnaise, 1 pint olive oil, 4 pints double cream, 3 pints yogurt, 2 pints self-raising flour, 1 pint tomato sauce, 40 avocado pears, 12 cloves garlic, 1 tsp. vanilla essence

and clean and take charge of children. You'd better ask them round. Don't be too smart, though. You don't want the women making those silly jokes about how they envy your wife; or the men getting pissed off behind your back. So you'd better be modest.

What will it be first? How about a lunchtime drinks party? You can repay absolutely everybody all at once and they'll all

talk to each other for most of the time. But this time we won't
invite the Footlings *or* the Smallcocks, they're just too
b.o.r.i.n.g. But the Footlings are great friends of the
Mogwoods, and we can't have the ones without the others.
And little Smallcock does feed the cat when we're stuck. But
last time we swore we'd just have the people we really liked.
Oh, well, ask them.

What will you serve? This is your chance to get rid of that
homemade wine. Are you sure? But it will cost a fortune
otherwise. Well, entertaining *is* expensive nowadays.

This dialogue is going on inside you. Let me get out the
homemade wine, you say. Not the wine you entered at the
Village Show last year? the other voice says. Yes, you say. You
mean the wine the judge took one look at and said: Dirty
bottle, you can tell a man made this, and then he uncorked it,
poured some out and said: Well, at least it glugs well.

Oh, all right, you growl. You abandon your better
judgement and go to the off licence to see if they have an
unassuming little Liebfraumilch on offer this week.

The guests arrive. You have been busy in the kitchen
putting blobs of pâté, cream cheese and garlic on savoury
biscuits. Your wife has been sauntering round smoking a cigar
and putting out the odd ashtray. You rush out of the kitchen
wiping your hands on your apron.

'Come in, come in!' you say merrily. 'Hello, Phyllis, hello,
Cyril. Hello, Miss Murdwick. Mind you don't slip on the
polished floor.'

'But, Charles!' they say. This is you. 'How absolutely lovely
everything looks.'

They move into the living room, carefully stepping round
one of your theme flower arrangements.

'What an *interesting* flower arrangement, Charles,' says Beryl
Mogwood. 'What does it represent?'

'Oh, it's a mere trifle, really,' you answer modestly. 'It
represents the triumph of youthful love over cant, hypocrisy
and false ideas.'

'Oh, I see,' she says. 'Shouldn't you take out the dead flowers?'

'Oh, no,' you say. 'They are the false ideas withering on the branch.'

'Good heavens,' she murmurs.

Suddenly she brightens.

'There's Felicity Footling!' she exclaims. 'I must go and say hello.'

When the guests leave little Miss Murdwick comes up to you. She holds your hand in hers. 'A lovely party,' she says. 'But your dear wife is looking tired. You mustn't let her work too hard.'

'I'll do my best,' you say in a jocular tone. 'Oops! Mind how you go. Very slippery floor since I tuned up the polisher.'

'Darling.' Your wife comes up to you. 'Will you get rid of Dave and Mave. They're your friends. They've opened another bottle and I want some lunch.'

Entertaining the wife's boss

The biggest challenge to the compleat man about the house is when your wife rings up at 6.00 p.m. and says she is bringing her boss home for dinner and can you prepare something really good this evening.

You sigh. You were looking forward to a quiet evening repairing the dog's basket. Brace up. Be a good husband. This could make all the difference to your wife's career.

Look at your watch. Five past six. The shops have just closed. What can you give them for dinner? Mentally you review your stores.

$1/2$ packet of fish fingers
1 slice of ham and 3 cold sausages
14 lb of onions

30 tins of meatballs
2 packets of jelly

Surely there's more than that? You'd better go and look.
Perhaps you could open some tins of meatballs, wash them,
make a sauce with some vegetable soup and garlic and serve
them as *roulades aux fines herbes du Général de Gaulle*.

Sit down and have a drink first. Plan the menu. This is
where the masculine touch comes in. This is the opportunity
for dedication to be crowned with inspiration. Slowly your eyes
turn towards the great basket of onions on the table. Perhaps
. . . yes. Your mind is working like lightning. And a pudding.
There'll have to be a pudding. And fortunately you've got
some wine left – your secret supply.

Purposefully, unhurriedly, with the confidence born of total
mastery, you set about your task. As you work you slot in a
cassette of a Vivaldi concerto.

Soon everything is ready. Have a sit down and read the
paper while you wait for them. You doze off.

You wake with a start when you hear a car. Is that them?
What time is it? Heavens, it's ten o'clock. The door opens and
a crowd of people pour in. However many of them are there?
They seem rather merry.

'Sorry we're a bit late, darling,' says your wife. 'The meeting
went on longer than expected.'

'Oh, hullo, everybody,' you say.

'Oh, yes,' says your wife. 'You know Paul, my boss. And
Bill, who handles overseas sales. This is Bill's friend Tina. And
this is Larry, from the States. He's visiting us at the moment.
And this is Larry's executive assistant, Sherry. This is my
husband, Charles, everyone.'

'Waal, hi, Charlie,' says Larry pleasantly. 'This is a really
great little house you have here.'

'It certainly is,' says Sherry. 'It's just wonderful to visit an
English home.'

You lead them through. In the dining room, the table is laid.
'I'll just set a few more places,' you murmur.

· 'Hey!' Larry is saying. 'Just look at this flower arrangement!'

Fig. 6. (below) is a suggested menu which (at a pinch) a man could serve to his wife's boss. Assuming there's not much in the house and you thought she was coming home on her own and stopping at the take-away anyway.

Menu

Danish open sandwiches avec thinly sliced
doigts de poisson

Vodka

—— ★ ——

Rice with diced saucisson froid et jambon

Woolworth Blanc de Blancs 1983

—— ★ ——

Onion surprise

—— ★ ——

Meatballs provençale

Réserve spéciale rouge maison

—— ★ ——

Poudingue anglais

—— ★ ——

Fromage Irish cheddar

—— ★ ——

Coffee

Rum

'Glad you noticed that,' you remark. 'It's the Empire State Building.'

Presently your wife's boss folds his napkin.

'What a delicious little supper that was,' he says, leaning towards your wife. He pats her hand, or perhaps her knee for all you know. '*So* kind of you to ask us.'

'This is a lovely pudding,' says someone.

'Oh, it's a mere trifle, really,' you answer modestly.

A loving atmosphere

More than anything, your family needs love. Never mind if you're hard up. Never mind if you're not terribly good at housework or cooking. Give your family lots of love and your rewards will be great. A man with a working wife should pay particular attention to this. He has so many opportunities to show that he cares.

For example, try leaving a note in the bed sometimes for your wife to discover. It could say 'PTO' on both sides, or 'You'll find your sandwiches down the bed', if you feel particularly humorous.

Another loving thing to do is to shampoo the dog, when everybody's out. To save water shampoo it in the bath with you.

And then, of course, you can save up out of your housekeeping money and buy her a little tiny something occasionally. A pot of her favourite yogurt.

And then you can do a little in the garden from time to time. Just keep it dug and manured and the grass cut. Don't try to do everything.

Best of all, of course, is planning the family holiday. The wife always has time to call at the travel agent and collect some brochures, so off you go and get them. While you're sitting a'one in the evening waiting for your wife to come home, you can pore over the endless vistas of concrete hotels, with swimming pools and guided tours of the old town only twenty miles away. Where should you go? The bazaars of Casablanca? The ruins of Crete? The orange groves of Sicily? The deserted beaches of Bulgaria?

How much is there in your reserve kitty? How many weeks' child allowance between now and July? Any bonuses due your wife? Any back tax?

Your head nods. The brochures fall on the floor. Sleep, O child of dreams.

10
Conclusion
or
The principle of enlightened self-interest

'No, no, no, no! You don't do it like that!'

You take your hand away. She relaxes and steps back.

You look at each other and shrug.

'You've got to communicate more tension!' shouts the producer. 'Remember you're looking for a scar. Really seize her! Do it again.'

This time you really seize her. The scene proceeds. Pity you don't know your lines.

'OK everybody,' says the producer. 'Let's do it once more.'

'Sorry,' you say. 'Can't stay too long. Had a problem getting a babysitter this evening.'

The count sidles up to you.

'Come on,' he says. 'A quick one in the Red Lion.'

'Really,' you say. 'I've had to leave the kids. Wife's working late . . . Oh well. Perhaps, a *very* quick one.'

You did it! You got away to a drama group rehearsal (and to the pub). Not easy, when a man has so much to do at home. How good to get away from children and housework and mix with adults and colleagues . . . How good to find your brain actually being taxed again.

Who said there isn't intellectual stimulus in running the house well? Well, there isn't. Not if you've got to do all the grot. A lot of work and not much reward in it.

Actually getting out for an evening and away from it all can be a major achievement. Now you know that not only are you busy all the time, but you don't even have the satisfaction of working steadily towards a particular goal, as you can (if you're ucky) in a job. In the house there's no such thing as an uninterrupted day. Bits of cleaning, bits of washing, transporting children, phone calls, getting meals. You can't settle down to anything.

It's very frustrating. You have to accept and adapt to it.

Types of wife

Naturally it all depends on what type of wife you've got.

Perhaps you're lucky. Perhaps your wife does find satisfaction in running the home and keeping things organised and cooking and looking after you. Perhaps she even tries to do this as well as go out and work. But are you really lucky to be waited on? Lazy and spoilt, more like.

Or perhaps your wife actually finds housework boring and the family ungrateful and the whole process of being at home stultifying and a drain of her energies in the best years of her life. Perhaps she has gifts which she can't express in the home. The need to go out and lead her own life can be strong. No wonder there are so many irritations and frustrations.

It's possible that you have a sly, humorous sort of wife. Perhaps she even read this book before you. You'll know if she did, because you'll find you are being served platefuls of unrecognisable but delicious mishmash at odd hours; or your shirts show signs of the five-stroke, not to say the two-stroke, technique; or you find strange flower arrangements in strange places; or a note in the bed saying, 'It's your turn.'

What has happened? Doesn't she care any more? Yes, she cares. But she's not taking it seriously.

Feminine and masculine

Most women, in common with females generally, have a nest-building instinct. Sometimes it comes out very strongly. Many mothers know that at the end of pregnancy, just when you would expect to be finally immobilised by bulk and discomfort, a strange manic passion comes over you and you begin to rearrange the house and do unseasonal spring cleaning. My wife went completely mad. She repapered the entire stairwell and teetered on the tops of ladders that, unpregnant, she wouldn't have dreamt of mounting. It was wonderful to get so much decorating done so quickly. Later we were surprised by the wallpaper chosen in the heat of the moment.

At ordinary times, the difference between the sexes is still apparent. Around the house and in the garden, you, the man, tend to undertake the structural, the architectural; you lay out the garden path or put in the bookshelves. Your wife creates the décor and the fertile lining; she bends over her seed beds, she attends to the furnishing and atmosphere of the home.

When a man takes over the running of the house and the care of the family he is, to some extent, going against nature. Instinct tends to work against a man having a natural concern for some of the housewifely ideals. The conditioning effect of our culture also militates against it. This makes it more difficult for you if you are going to spend your time at home.

There are cases where role reversal seems to work very well: the wife goes out and earns money, the husband runs the home. It depends on the couple. Perhaps in your case you just want to lend a hand; perhaps your wife is handicapped; perhaps you are the worm that is turning from the drudgery of commuting and or the office routine; perhaps you are unemployed; perhaps the two of you simply share the burden.

Your wife shouldn't expect you to bring a woman's instincts to bear. Men bring something else: a different kind of energy, indifference to things which many women consider important, a wonderful talent for short cats. Sorry, cuts.

At least you're well equipped now, if you've glanced at some of the preceding pages. You have some of the basic skills and techniques at your fingertips . . . You may even have observed the principle of enlightened self-interest: you usually reap what you sow. Or the world tends to treat you in the way that you treat it.

By now you should have a healthy perspective on running homes and families. Care, but don't take things too seriously. Who wants to live in a nice clean house and be miserable? For that matter, who wants to live in a scruffy house and be miserable?

OK, you men can say to your wives. Go out and make your way in the world; you can leave the rest to us. Get out from under our feet! Eat your hearts out, working women.

Viv Quillan
Taking the Lid off Kids £1.50

What starts as a twinkle in father's eye, becomes an expected happy event and ends up as *a kid*. Kids. They are all here, from the Accumulator who hoards secondhand chewing gum and dead birds, to the Zombie, comatose in front of the television, emerging only to check for spots and split ends. An A–Z of Kids, guaranteed non-fiction.

Robert Walker
First Clue £2.50
the A–Z of finding out

This invaluable addition to any reference shelf will direct you to the best way of finding the answer to any one of hundreds of queries. Thoroughly researched, carefully planned and up to date, it tells you which organization to contact and what their address/phone number is, and which book or magazine will give you further information – whether you need an accountant, want to join a union, organize travel abroad or find the nearest club for your favourite sport.

Fritz Spiegl
Keep Taking the Tabloids £1.50

Exclusive – Spiegl On the Street! Meaning a survey by Fritz Spiegl of the contribution to contemporary popular culture made by the denizens of Fleet Street. *Keep Taking the Tabloids* shows the World According to the Hacks. A place where everyone not *hitting out* is *appealing*, where price increases are *slapped on* to make *costs soar*, where every ambulance is making a *mercy dash* and every inflamed chip pan is a *fire drama*. *Vice probe horror shock – bishop named* is an effective way to sell papers. So that's the way the industry is run. Now in these *exclusive and revealing* pages Spiegl shows you how it's done. . .

Christopher Ward
Our Cheque is in the Post £1.50

A book of excuses from the author of *How to Complain*.

Reasons for not helping with the washing up. . .being late, leaving early;
excuses for being drunk. . .avoiding dancing or sex; convincing things to tell
policemen and what to do if you are caught out telling a lie'
DAILY TELEGRAPH

Very useful some of these tips are. Reason you didn't telephone when you
promised you would: one of the children snipped through the cable with
wire clippers' KEITH WATERHOUSE, DAILY MIRROR

Brian Moynahan
Fool's Paradise £1.75

A tricks-of-the-trade guide to the great international tourist rip-off, explaining
who gets rich from the tourist industry and how they do it – from the travel
agent's rake-off to the souvenir seller's split. Credit card rackets, the hotel
is a round-the-clock money machine, package tour profiteers and coach
rides that are just a dice game with death. . .The author of *Airport
International* takes a long hard look at the tourist industry worldwide.

Nicholas Parsons
Dipped in Vitriol £1.75

A hilarious survey of hatchet reviews of the arts through the epochs –
vitriolic offerings from Clive James, Bernard Levin, Gore Vidal, Oscar Wilde,
Richard Ingrams, the *Sun*, *Pravda*, George Bernard Shaw and many more.

Perception of badness, as of beauty, is in the eye of the beholder. . .This is
a humorous excursion through the realms of badness, highlighting self-
importance in autobiography, pretentiousness and incompetence in fiction,
mountebankery and shallowness in theatre, whimsical follies in music, brain-
crushing false goods in cinema. . .'

Barbara Grigson
The Home Herbal £1.95
a handbook of simple remedies

As people increasingly turn to alternative medicines and therapies here is an authoritative and practical guide to herbal remedies, for a whole range of minor medical problems and ailments where conventional medicine may fail to provide relief or produce unpleasant side-effects. The book is organized alphabetically under the medical problems from acne to whooping cough, suggesting herbal remedies, where to get them and how to use them. Additional chapters cover the preparation of medicines, where to find your herbs, stocks of herbs for family needs, common and Latin botanical names.

Gail Duff
Country Wisdom £1.75

An encyclopedia of recipes, remedies and traditional good sense. The popular author of *Vegetarian Cookbook* and *Fresh all the Year* has collected pages and pages of fascinating folklore, herbal recipes, traditional advice culled from centuries of country life. Cures for everything from insomnia to toothache, hints for home and kitchen, traditional good sense and entertainment on every page.

Jancis Robinson
Masterglass £2.95
a practical course in wine tasting

This is a book for all those who want to know more about wine, but already know that drinking it is much more interesting than reading about it.

It explains how wine is made, what factors influence taste, and how to get every possible pleasure from drinking it. Side by side with all this necessary information is a practical course in developing tasting skills.

Masterglass shows you how to drink your way to a real knowledge of wine.

Fiction

]	**Options**	Freda Bright	£1.50p
]	**The Thirty-nine Steps**	John Buchan	£1.50p
]	**Secret of Blackoaks**	Ashley Carter	£1.50p
]	**Hercule Poirot's Christmas**	Agatha Christie	£1.25p
]	**Dupe**	Liza Cody	£1.25p
]	**Lovers and Gamblers**	Jackie Collins	£2.50p
]	**Sphinx**	Robin Cook	£1.25p
]	**Ragtime**	E. L. Doctorow	£1.50p
]	**My Cousin Rachel**	Daphne du Maurier	£1.95p
]	**Mr American**	George Macdonald Fraser	£2.25p
]	**The Moneychangers**	Arthur Hailey	£2.25p
]	**Secrets**	Unity Hall	£1.75p
]	**Black Sheep**	Georgette Heyer	£1.75p
]	**The Eagle Has Landed**	Jack Higgins	£1.95p
]	**Sins of the Fathers**	Susan Howatch	£2.95p
]	**The Master Sniper**	Stephen Hunter	£1.50p
]	**Smiley's People**	John le Carré	£1.95p
]	**To Kill a Mockingbird**	Harper Lee	£1.95p
]	**Ghosts**	Ed McBain	£1.75p
]	**Gone with the Wind**	Margaret Mitchell	£3.50p
]	**Blood Oath**	David Morrell	£1.75p
]	**Platinum Logic**	Tony Parsons	£1.75p
]	**Wilt**	Tom Sharpe	£1.75p
]	**Rage of Angels**	Sidney Sheldon	£1.95p
]	**The Unborn**	David Shobin	£1.50p
]	**A Town Like Alice**	Nevile Shute	£1.75p
]	**A Falcon Flies**	Wilbur Smith	£1.95p
]	**The Deep Well at Noon**	Jessica Stirling	£1.95p
]	**The Ironmaster**	Jean Stubbs	£1.75p
]	**The Music Makers**	E. V. Thompson	£1.95p

Non-fiction

]	**Extraterrestrial Civilizations**	Isaac Asimov	£1.50p
]	**Pregnancy**	Gordon Bourne	£2.95p
]	**Jogging From Memory**	Rob Buckman	£1.25p
]	**The 35mm Photographer's Handbook**	Julian Calder and John Garrett	£5.95p
]	**Travellers' Britain**	Arthur Eperon	£2.95p
]	**Travellers' Italy**		£2.50p
]	**The Complete Calorie Counter**	Eileen Fowler	75p

All these books are available at your local bookshop or newsagent, or can be ordered direct from the publisher. Indicate the number of copies required and fill in the form below

9

....

Name_____
(Block letters please)

Address_____

_____

Send to Pan Books (CS Department), Cavaye Place, London SW10 9PG
Please enclose remittance to the value of the cover price plus:
35p for the first book plus 15p per copy for each additional book ordered
to a maximum charge of £1.25 to cover postage and packing
Applicable only in the UK

While every effort is made to keep prices low, it is sometimes
necessary to increase prices at short notice. Pan Books reserve
the right to show on covers and charge new retail prices which
may differ from those advertised in the text or elsewhere